ABIEGAIL ROSE

Prince, Not Required

Fix your crown, slay your inner dragons, and unlock your authentic self to understand the value you bring to the world!

PUBLICATIONS

Second edition

ISBN: 978-1086634778

Cover art by Abiegail Rose
Illustration by G_Pink - Adobe Stock
Editing by Rhonda Riley

This book was professionally typeset on Reedsy.
Find out more at reedsy.com

This book is dedicated to the amazing group of women that I have the pleasure of working with! We always get the job done, but I never feel like I'm working. Kendra, Heather T., Jaclyn, Heather S., Nicole, Rachel, Rachael, and Cori. You are all truly so inspiring!

Contents

IX   A Journey Completed

Acknowledgement

I have to start by thanking my awesome son, Solomon. You are a constant motivation to put my crown on each day, so that I can lead by example in all that I do.

Thank you to my mom you were such an amazing help. From reading early drafts, to giving me advice on the cover, to keeping Solomon occupied so I could edit. She was as important to this book getting done as I was. Thank you so much!

Thanks to everyone on the Boss Babe Publications team who stood with me as I started our small but flourishing publishing company.

Introduction

Welcome Queen!

Prince Not Required is a book that is solely focused on you!

This book has 4 main goals. For you to...

- Fix your crown,
- Slay your inner dragons,
- Unlock your authentic self, and to
- Understand the value you bring to the world

Along the way you'll learn many things about yourself and how you can find the courage to confidently wear your self-love crown and proudly show the world the real you. Your journey ends in an exciting vision of a future that you design yourself, based on your own goals, dreams, and passions.

Remember: No two palaces are alike!

Your journey to true authenticity includes:

1. Getting to know the queen inside
2. Giving yourself a queenly self-concept makeover
3. Accepting your throne
4. Wearing your self-love crown proudly
5. Determining your role as monarch
6. Discovering your queenly authenticity

Benefiting From Your Journey

How to Get the Most Out of This Book and Online Course

This book and the online course is packed with lessons and they're all sequential. So, it's important that you start at the beginning and do each lesson in order, without skipping any.

If you're ready to get started, go to queenly.thinkific.com and you'll find directions for logging in at the back of the book.

Take the time to practice the action tips that you find in each lesson. Some of these tips are things to reflect on and some of them are ideas to try out. Please keep an open mind and try them all. Then, you can determine which tips work the best for you and continue working with those.

Please note that there are Affirmations and Self-Reflections in the e-course for each lesson as well. The online course has additional materials that help you in whatever task you are working on in that lesson. *Every lesson has something extra for you!* You could find articles, affirmations, action guides, or a workbook.

How to Use the Affirmations

You'll find quite a few affirmations/reflections throughout Prince, Not Required!

Did you know that affirmations have the power to change your thoughts, self-talk, and ultimately, your actions?

They can strengthen your talents and help you develop traits that you wish to learn. They can enable you to overpower negative thoughts with positive ones.

You can use them just as you find them in the resources section, or you can further customize them for your own circumstances. In fact, it would work well for you to even write your own! Writing your own affirmations will make them extremely personal to you, making them most effective.

Wondering how to write an affirmation? No worries! *You'll find a helpful guide for writing your own affirmations coming up next.* Try writing a few. You might discover a new talent!

Affirmations work the best when you repeat them to yourself several times a day. If you make up some short ones like the guide shows you, you can repeat these positive statements each time that you feel stress during the day and could use a "pick-me-up."

Soon, you'll notice the positive queenly changes you desire!

Enjoy!

Have fun with this book and the course. Practice each lesson and repeat each affirmation as much as you need to, before you go on to the next step in your journey to queenly authenticity.

Remember: It's not a race, it's a strut down a long red carpet.

Have a great trip!

1

Getting to Know the Queen Inside

The first step to discovering queenly authenticity is to find out who you really are. So, our path begins with helping you to discover your inner dragons and develop self-awareness. You'll discover many details about your personality and how you got that way. We'll also discuss how your past experiences have influenced you and help you clarify your values and true passions.

Queenly Affirmations

How to Write Your Own Affirmations

*A*ffirmations are everywhere, and they have the strong ability to **lift your spirits to get through hard times.** This is because we're all highly suggestible, even if we think we're not!

Affirmations help us to keep a positive attitude about life. It's only natural that we'll get more out of these positive sayings if we formulate them ourselves. Writing our own affirmations makes them personal to us, which can then help us to get through our own individual situations.

When you start writing your own affirmations, keep these tips in mind:

Make them personal. When you write affirmations, it's important to remember to use *"I"* in them. They *are* personal to *you* after all.
　　Example: *"I am having an exceptional day today!"*

Use the present tense. Affirmations are built in order to change our feelings *now*, which is why you want to stay positive and strong in this moment. When you use the past tense, you get nostalgic. When you use the future tense, you get hopeful. The present tense helps you feel the difference right now.
　　Example: *"I am feeling relaxed."*

Be down to earth. This just means to use your own style and try not to make your affirmations too formal or wishy-washy. You want to capture your own voice.
　　Bad Example: *"Presently I feel the urge to enjoy my existence."*
　　Good Example: *"I enjoy my life."*

Be short. Affirmations are meant to be short, simple and sweet. Stay on target and make your affirmation a one-liner. If it's too wordy, try breaking it up into a few affirmations. ***The trick is to stick with one simple idea at a time.***
　　Example: *"I am in perfect health."*

Make it positive. Affirmations are positive statements, so avoid negative words like *"not."* You're using affirmations to make a life improvement and positive statements motivate you to make this improvement.
　　Example: *"I am at peace with my mind."*

Make it believable. You don't want your affirmation to sound like something out of this world. If it's not believable, you won't take it seriously and your subconscious will just dismiss it.

Example: *"I am choosing to be happy today."*

Believe in the Power of Affirmations

When you say your affirmations, ***believe them to be true.*** Affirmations are truly powerful sets of words as long as you believe what you're telling yourself.

Affirmations alone have been known to help people cure addictions. Women even use them during childbirth to help them stay calm and collected during natural delivery.

First, set your eyes on your goal and then write your affirmations to get yourself there.

Write Them Down

Practice always makes perfect. Write down the affirmations you're feeling. Then go over the list above and make sure that your affirmations follow the rules. Once they do, start using your affirmations and feel the difference. ***Say your affirmations to yourself daily.*** Take deep breaths and keep your eyes on your goal.

Also if need be, tweak your affirmations. These positive sayings aren't written in stone, so as you change, your affirmations can change, too.

It's best to keep your affirmations in a place where you can see them. You can simply keep a list in your pocket or you can post them around the house. Paste them on the bathroom mirror, on your computer, or wherever you know you'll see them each day.

Affirmations can make all the difference in reaching your goals. Give them a try and enjoy the benefits these positive statements can make in your life.

Know Yourself

The First Step to Queenly Authenticity

*I*t's impossible to live authentically without first discovering who you are. Self-awareness is crucial! This first module will help you discover yourself.

What is self-awareness? The dictionary defines self-awareness as "knowledge and awareness of your own personality or character." **When you're self-aware, you have an accurate and clear understanding of your personality, strengths, weaknesses, and beliefs.** You know what makes you tick. Self-awareness also includes an understanding of how others perceive you.

Lacking self-awareness can lead to a very confusing and frustrating life!

Your level of self-awareness can influence your relationships, career, and happiness:

Self-awareness is necessary for taking control of your life.
The direction of your life is determined by your thoughts, beliefs,
emotions, and reactions. Self-awareness is the principle way of
understanding and influencing these things.

- *Self-awareness highlights faulty beliefs and emotional reactions that stand in your way and gives you the power to make adjustments.*

**Self-awareness illuminates the real reasons for past failures
and challenges.** We often dismiss our failures as bad luck or a lack
of proper timing. But it's also possible that we failed to perceive the
situation, others, or ourselves accurately. It's much easier to see the
reason behind relationship, work, and other struggles when we can
look at ourselves clearly.

- Do you consistently struggle at work or in your relationships? What can you do better?

- Those who lack self-awareness are puzzled by their negative outcomes or blame others exclusively.

Self-awareness is a critical quality for leaders. One study con-
cluded that *a high degree of self-awareness was the best predictor of
success for executives.*

- Executives that have an understanding of their weaknesses are able to build a team composed of members that fill those weaknesses.

- A lack of self-awareness puts a limit on your leadership abilities.

Self-awareness is the foundation for personal progress. Without it, any personal development efforts will be severely hampered.

- Self-awareness is the cornerstone of success and self-improvement. Without self-awareness, the knowledge you possess can't be applied effectively. It's necessary to understand your beliefs, habits, strengths, and weaknesses to make a personal change. Avoid assuming that you're self-aware. Give it some time and thought.

Building greater self-awareness won't happen overnight, but it can be developed. You can start building your self-awareness, and reaping the benefits, starting today!

Your next lesson gives you 10 ways to develop queenly self-awareness. But before you tackle dancing with that dragon log-in to your course online and read the affirmations for this lesson and answer the self-reflection questions:

- I discover more about myself each day
- I have a clear understanding of who I am

Here's what you need to do today:

Make a list of your daily habits and mark each habit as positive or negative.

Then pick just *one* habit to work on. It can be a positive habit that you want to develop further, or you can pick a negative habit that you want to change. Make a plan for changing your chosen habit.

Develop Queenly Self-Awareness

To recap from your last lesson, self-awareness is having a high degree of knowledge about yourself. *It's awareness of your habits, emotional tendencies, needs, desires, strengths, and weaknesses.* Having a high level of self-awareness is a powerful tool. It allows you to change your life more effectively, since you know how you tick. Those that lack self-awareness find life to be frustrating.

Develop your self-awareness:

1. **Notice your thoughts.** Unless you've been meditating for years, your mind is constantly churning through ideas and endlessly providing commentary. You can't just look at a tree and admire it, your mind has to comment, "That's a beautiful tree." Then it's off to the races.

   - Notice your thinking patterns. What are you thinking when you're feeling nervous? Bored? Interested? Walking down the street? *Notice that similar situations result in similar thought patterns.*

11

- Do you judge people and situations? Do you spend a lot of time thinking about the past or the future? Do you expect the worst to happen or the best? Or do you adopt an attitude of, *"Let's just see what happens"*?

2. **Notice your feelings.** What are you feeling throughout the day? What do you feel while you're eating? Driving to work? Lying in bed? Waiting in line?

- Once you've notice your emotion, question it. What am I feeling? Why? What do I need right now? How do I normally react in this situation? Is that smart?

3. **Understand how you deal with frustration or emotional discomfort.** *A huge chunk of your time is spent trying to make yourself feel better.* If you feel slightly frustrated or uncomfortable, then you may spend a tremendous amount of time and energy trying to change the situation or the others around you to resolve those negative feelings.

- Do you try to control others? Do you attempt to distract yourself? Is your first instinct to leave the situation? Do you surf the internet or eat a big bowl of ice cream?

4. **Examine your friendships.** Where do you find your friends? Are most of your friendships long-term or short? When your friendships

end, what is the common cause? What types of people do you prefer to be friends with? What types of people do you avoid?

5. **Examine your intimate relationships.** Do you see a pattern in the type of people that you've been involved with? What are the negative characteristics they all share? Why do you think those people appealed to you?

- What were your shortcomings in your relationships? Are you clingy? Jealous? Too focused on work? Failed to communicate your needs? Think about how you contributed to the failure of your relationships.

- Have you changed your approach from relationship to relationship, or do you continue to repeat your mistakes?

6. **Keep a journal.** There's no better way to learn about yourself than to record your thoughts, feelings, and experiences each day. *Studies have shown that we don't remember our past very accurately, so record it while it's still fresh in your mind.* Be sure to include your high and low points for the day.

- Note how well you ate and slept, too. You might find some useful information.

- Create a habit of writing in your journal for at least 15 minutes each day. You'll start to notice patterns and learn a lot about yourself.

13

7. **Write your own manifesto.** *Think about and then document your views on life, your goals, and your intentions.* You might be surprised by what you write. This is a great first step for understanding yourself and your beliefs.

8. **Make a list of your strengths and weaknesses.** How do you know? Are you certain? Avoid jumping to conclusions. You may have always believed that you're a hard worker, but are you? To whom are you comparing yourself? Provide yourself with proof before you make any decisions.

9. **What would others say about you?** Consider how your partner, children, friends, family, co-workers, and boss would describe you. What would they suggest you improve about yourself? Then ask them and see how accurate you are. Do you know how others perceive you? Find out how perceptive you are.

10. **Meditate.** Meditation is all about developing a better awareness of the present moment and yourself. *Meditation is an ideal activity for enhancing self-awareness.*

- Meditate at least once each day. Spend the rest of the day paying attention to yourself, others, and your surroundings. You can develop a higher degree of self-awareness by just paying attention.

- Question yourself throughout the day. *"What am I attempting to achieve?" "What emotions am I currently feeling and why?" "What are the people around me feeling?"*

Understanding yourself might be the most important part of becoming and living authentically. The next lesson guides you through pondering your personal identity. But before we go to far into our journey lets take some time to Affirm & Reflect like every real Queen should. Login to your course and complete the affirmation and reflection questions for this lesson:

- Increasing Self Awareness
- Meditation teaches me about myself.

Here's what you need to do today:

Spend the rest of the day noticing your feelings. Do you see patterns emerging in similar situations?

Pondering Your Queenly Identity

Who Are You?

*I*n the last couple of lessons, you started to expand your knowledge of yourself. Who you are—your identity—is a powerful force in your life and speaks volumes to others who come into contact with you. Your personal identity includes more than just your thoughts and feelings. Today, we look at some other things that help make up your personal identity.

Your identity plays an important role in your kingdom (decisions and relationships).

Thinking about who you are will strengthen the connections among your mind, body, and behaviors. Also, you can get a better handle of where you are in life as well as where you're headed.

Although there are plenty of psychological theories out there about identity, including its formation and how you maintain it, consider these basic elements of your identity:

1. **Your personal family history.** *Where you were raised, who you grew up with, and the experiences you had as you matured from an infant all the way through your early adult years are powerful factors affecting the development of your personal identity.*

- Consider sayings like, "You can take the girl out of the city, but you can't take the city out of the girl" and their implications. In essence, where you've come from plays a major role in who you are.

- That being said, your history doesn't have to be the end of the story when it comes to your present identity. An encouraging thing about life is that you can take steps to be the person you want to be at any time.

2. **The "group" of people you hang out with.** Much of who you are today can be attributed to the people you most closely affiliate with. Your friends probably share interests in the same kinds of things you find fascinating.

- Think about it—perhaps several of your girlfriends are into crafting and so are you. You're into yoga and a bit of a health nut as are a few of your best gal pals. Even though you may associate the idea of "cliques" with your teen years, it's still true that we gravitate towards people who we share similarities with.

- As with the first point, you can be selective about the people you choose to hang out with. If you want to be studious, you can look for others who spend time in libraries and taking classes. If you want to be successful, choose to hang out with people you view as good at their work and successful in life.

3. **Your physical appearance.** The clothes you choose to wear, the hairstyle you have, and how you conduct yourself physically combine to make up an important aspect of your personal identity. Although your appearance isn't the only thing that's relevant about who you are, the fact is that your physical state provides people with a picture of who you are.

4. **Your feelings, thoughts, and beliefs about you.** Your self-image is made up of how you feel about yourself as an individual. Also, what you believe to be true about yourself is a powerful force in determining your personal identity.

- For example, if you believe you're an overweight, unattractive person, then you might unconsciously portray those character-istics toward others. But if you see yourself as someone who's working hard to excel in her career and willing to give something to get something, you present a more positive identity to others.

- What you feel, think, and believe about yourself are major aspects of your overall identity.

Make it a point to ponder who you are as an individual human being on this earth. Recognize that your personal identity is a complex mix of your history, your affiliations, and your thoughts and beliefs about yourself. How you appear to others is also representative of your identity.

Realize that you have considerable power to influence the type of identity you possess and show to others. As you develop your authenticity, stay true to who you really are. However, you can still learn to let go of the negative influences of the past that inhibit you today.

The next lesson talks about your past and how writing down past episodes of your life can help you in your quest to get to know yourself. But before you jump in pencil hot and ready or fingers itching to type let's have you log-in and complete this lesson's affirmation and reflection questions.

- I Embrace My Identity
- My Career is Separate from My Identity

Here's what you need to do today:

List 3 best friends that you hang out with the most. How do these friends affect your identity?

Understand Your Inner Queen

Journaling Your Life

*I*n the last lesson, we talked about your queenly identity. Do you feel like you don't understand your own motives or choices? If you feel this way, you can learn why you do the things you do.

One method to increase self-understanding is journaling your thoughts and feelings.

The idea of keeping a journal may sound strange to you; you might not think of yourself as a writer. Even non-writers keep journals, though. When you open yourself to journaling, you experience a new wealth of self-understanding.

Writing bits and pieces of your life experiences can be an incredible journey. Once you start thinking about something that happened to you in the past, you'll find yourself remembering another story, then another.

Once you start making an effort to recall experiences from your past, you'll trigger memories you haven't thought about in years.

All of the experiences you'll recall have combined to make you the person you are. To sort back through some of your life stories will help you understand yourself so much more.

Follow these steps to get started:

1. **Decide how you'll write your story.** Will you use a spiral notebook and a pen? A computer is the obvious choice if you're comfortable with it.

2. **Don't worry about starting at the beginning.** Interestingly, a lot of people avoid trying to write down stories of their lives because they "can't remember back that far." ***Where you start the story isn't important. Starting it is.***

3. **Think of your life as a series of short chapters.** To simplify your story, each situation you recall can be a "chapter." For example, you might remember the time your Aunt Cindy took you to the park and you fell off the slide. Go directly to your computer, open up a blank document and start typing.

4. **Focus on getting the story down.** *Things like sentence structure, spelling, grammar, and the like aren't all that important for now, unless you plan to publish your journal.* You can deal with all those things later by going back through and editing the material.

5. **The order of your stories is irrelevant.** There are two suggested ways to do your stories on the computer:

- Open a new document for each "chapter" and title the document to describe the story.

- Or simply write all your stories in one document. Open that document when you feel like writing a story and separate the stories by using chapter headings.

- If you feel the need later on, you can copy and paste the stories into whatever order you like.

6. **Document what you remember.** Get down information about what happened, what you did, what you thought, and how you felt. These details will ultimately lead you to develop a better understanding of how you've lived your life as an adult.

Writing your life story is not all that difficult. If you follow some of these journaling methods and keep your focus off of the end result, you'll find yourself recalling more and more parts of your life. Plus, you'll learn to understand and even love yourself more than you ever have!

There's still more of you to get to know too! Consider your personal values and passions. The next lesson will help you identify your personal values. However, before we go further down of the path let's login to the course and complete this lesson's affirmation and self-reflection questions:

- My journal teaches me about myself.

Here's what you need to do today:

Get a spiral notebook, blank journal, or open your word processor on your computer, then pick a story from your life and write it down. Include your thoughts and feelings about this experience. How does the experience affect who you are today?

Establishing Your Queenly Values

❧◦❧

So far in this course, we've been guiding you through discovering who you really are. ***One way to truly know yourself is to get in touch with your own set of values.***

It's easy to get distracted by others' ideals and claim that they're your own because of certain pressures. However, it's vital that you have your *own* set of principles and morals so you can stand firm in your beliefs.

Your values are simply the things that are most important to you at the core. It's the unwavering belief in what you stand for. When you know your values, you can live an authentic life doing what's most important to you.

Expanding Your Mind Through Visualizations

An effective method of identifying your values is to imagine your future. Take the time to reflect on different areas of your life. Where do you see yourself as you get older? What are the things that are most important to you? What do you hope to accomplish in life?

Answering these questions will help you discover your values. For instance, if you picture yourself growing old close to your family and spending valuable time with your grandkids, then a strong sense of family is one of your core values.

You can have many values in life; you just need to discover which ones are your highest priorities. That way, at the end of each day, *you can feel confident that you're nurturing the most important parts of your life.*

Popular Values

There are certain values that most people feel are important. You might find that they're significant to you too, as part of your core beliefs.

These values may help guide you in determining your own personal values:

1. **Adventure.** Are you a thrill-seeker? If things seem to get too stale, do you eventually feel bored? If so, you have adventure close to your heart and you'd be happiest with trying new experiences and new ways of doing everyday things.

2. **Relationships.** Valuing relationships includes finding *all* relationships important, in addition to your romantic ones. If you value loving relationships, it might be those with any family member or friend. This means that you hold your interactions with your loved ones to be one of the most important things in life.

3. **Spirituality.** If you align with a certain religion or spiritual practice, then the beliefs of that practice are likely dear to your heart. You may find greater fulfillment by spending your time studying and practicing your spiritual explorations.

4. **Creativity.** Creative thinking helps the world in many ways, but it's not a core value for everyone. If you enjoy discovering and creating new things, perhaps it *is* one of *your* values. Try thinking outside the box while you're doing things that you enjoy, such as poetry, music, or painting.

5. **Making a mark on the world.** Most people will say that, in the end, they just want others to warmly remember them. There are many ways that you can make your mark on the world, if that's one of your core values. You can help others through volunteer work, you can create something new to help the world at large, or you can be a positive influence on others, and much more.

All you really need to do in order to discover your values is find what makes you *truly* happy. ***Then ask yourself why those things bring you joy.*** The answers will lead you to your core values.

If you feel like your life has taken a wrong turn, you can figure it all out by thinking about your future. Are you helping your future self by walking down your current path? If the answer is no, perhaps it's time to think about taking a new path based on your core values. When you do, that path will likely lead you to happiness!

The things and activities that you're passionate about are closely related to your core values. The next lesson takes you through 15 questions that can help you discover your passions. Before that login to the course to Affirm and Reflect on this lesson:

• My Values Shape My Destiny

Here's what you need to do today:

In your journal, write down 3 things that make you truly happy. Why do these things bring you joy? The answer will likely lead you to some core values!

Discover Your Queenly Passions

~~~

One of the most exciting parts of living authentically as a queen is getting to design your life around the things you love most! In the last lesson, we talked about your values. Today, we'll add your passions to your quest for self-discovery.

If you're lucky, you've already discovered your passions in life and have devoted much of your life to fulfilling dreams and goals related to things that bring excitement and joy.

However, maybe you've not yet connected with activities, skills, and interests that ignite your passion. It takes time, soul-searching, and some life experience to identify your true passions. So, to get your thoughts, ideas, and desires flowing, explore the following questions.

These prompts will help you tap into your wants, needs, desires, and fantasies. Have fun with them. Who knows? *By the time you reach the end of these questions, you may have identified your true passions!*

1. **What's the one thing I've always wanted to do since I was a child?** If you still want to do it, explore what would need to happen

in order for you to carry through with this long-sought wish.

2. If I could spend today doing whatever I wanted, what would I be doing? Let your mind go. It could be something related to your work, your home, or simply a lark.

3. Where do I really want to live—the city and the type of residence? Perhaps you're already fulfilling this passion and you do live in your true first choice. If not, ponder the possibilities of moving to a place you'll love.

4. What is something I would like to explore that no one knows about? Perhaps you're harboring a secret yearning to visit Washington, D.C. or Westminster Abbey in London. The streets of Hong Kong may be calling your name or even the Grand Canyon. Can you make it happen?

5. What do I talk about doing but never do, or even take any steps toward completing the wish? In a conversation, you might state something like, "For the last 10 years, I've really wanted to take a cruise to the Caribbean."

6. What are my reasons for not going after my dreams? It's time to explore within yourself why you haven't pursued the life you want.

7. How will I finish the sentence, "More than anything, before I die, I want to _____?" Say it out loud and fill in the blank. Then, figure out a way to accomplish your wish.

8. What are the things in my life that I would like to get rid of? If you're discovering you don't love everything about your life, maybe it's time to do some "housecleaning." Make a list of the ways you'd like your life to change.

9. Which people in my life inspire me and why? *It's important to know who inspires you so you can spend more time with them.* What is it about them that lights you up so much? Decide to take every step to get inspired more often. You'll find your passions this way.

10. If I were to make just one radical change in my life right now to make life better, what would it be? Your answer to this question will really open up your possibilities. Moving to a bigger city might really spice up your life. Getting more education might be a goal—plus you'll likely make more money.

- You'll be happier if you chase your dreams. Make 1 change.

11. How do I feel when I put all my effort into accomplishing a goal I've chosen? Notice these feelings. You'll no doubt want to experience them more often.

12. How do I feel whenever I achieve a life goal? Awesome, probably.

13. What's missing from my life? Answering this question requires considerable soul-searching.

14. Who are my biggest supporters? It's wise to know the people that will stand behind you and help you pursue your passions, no matter what.

15. Who gets in the way of me achieving my goals? In order to find your true passions, you might be required to disengage from those who are dragging you down.

If you take the time to thoroughly ponder each of these questions, you'll be pleased with what you find. Your true passions are just waiting to be discovered!

Finding your passions is one of the most enjoyable tasks in learning to live authentically. Knowing your passions helps clarify your self-concept. However, there are several more things that work together to form your self-concept. In the next part of your journey to authenticity, you'll get to give yourself a self-concept makeover.

But first, we'll pause and login to the course for summary and reflection.

- How Finding Your Passion Can Improve Your Life
- How to Become More Passionate

Here's what you need to do today:

In your journal, write down your answers to these 15 questions. Continue to brainstorm and write down any more passions that come to mind.

Your Queenly Reflection

T he first step to being authentic is to know yourself – to develop your self-awareness. You can become more self-aware by taking note of your thoughts, feelings, strengths and weaknesses. Examine your friendships and intimate relationships. Discovering what others think of you can add to your self-awareness as well.

Look at your past and analyze how it affects your present circumstances, beliefs, and values. Make your own decision as to how you want it to affect your future.

Discover your passions by delving into many areas of things you enjoy the most.

Learn strategies to develop and maintain your self-awareness. Meditating and writing a journal both are effective aids in this endeavor.

The more self-aware you become, the more authentically you'll be able to live your life. Login to the course and complete this lessons affirmations:

- I am secure in my sense of self.
- I discover new strengths each day.

Self-Reflection Questions:

1. Why do I need to be self-aware in order to live authentically?

2. Do I feel like I've been self-aware in the past? How can learning more about myself help me?

3. How does my childhood affect my current beliefs? How does it affect my values?

4. What parts of my childhood do I want to carry with me into the future? What experiences do I want to let go of?

5. What can I learn about myself from my friends?

6. What are my passions? How can I structure my life so that more of my daily activities reflect these passions?

Moving forward, part 2 enables you to give yourself a queenly self-concept makeover!

The Queen Inside Quiz

***

This quiz is available as apart of your Thinkific Course. Just visit queenly.thinkific.com, login, and choose the correct answers.

1. You'll get the most from this course if you:

- a. Choose lessons based on personal interest
- b. Do the lessons in sequential order
- c. Look at the quiz first and then do the lessons
- d. Quickly read through each lesson and do the quiz

2. Affirmations have the power to:

- a. Hypnotize you
- b. Convince someone to go on a date
- c. Change your life, one thought at a time
- d. Nothing. They don't do anything.

3. What will you find in the online course for each lesson?

- a. Links to other products that can help you
- b. Links to other websites that can help you
- c. Extra content that helps you learn the lesson
- d. None of the above

4. What is the foundation for personal progress?

- a. Self-awareness
- b. Self-criticism
- c. Self-Assurance
- d. Self-Control

5. What is an ideal activity for enhancing self-awareness?

- a. Meditation
- b. Sleeping
- c. Studying another language
- d. Watching TV

6. Which of these aspects are included in your personal identity?

- a. Your personal family history
- b. Your physical appearance
- c. The people you hang out with
- d. All of the above

7. Keeping a journal can increase your self-understanding.

- a. True
- b. False

8. Discovering your passions means you can:

- a. Finally go on a date
- b. Design your life around the things you love most
- c. Call in sick to work tomorrow
- d. Watch TV

9. Which of the following questions can help you identify your passions?

- a. What's missing from my life?
- b. What am I good at?
- c. What activities did I like when I was a child?
- d. All of the above

10. What are your values?

- a. The ideas that are most important to you
- b. Your favorite TV show

- c. Your jewelry, money, and other high-priced items
- d. All of the above

II

Give Yourself a Queenly Self-Concept Makeover

What goes into forming your self-concept? Are the things you believe about yourself really true? It's hard to have queenly authenticity if you have mistaken beliefs about yourself! Part 2 takes you through the steps to give yourself a self-concept makeover any queen would have dragons slayed for. It helps you to re-evaluate your past, form a healthy self-concept, and build your self-esteem.

Evaluating Dragons

ᴈᴖᴧᴖᴧᴖᴐ

Now that we've finished part one, you must know a lot about yourself!

Congratulations, Queen!

However, knowing yourself means having accurate beliefs about yourself. This may be hard to take in, but *it's entirely possible that some of the things you believe about yourself aren't true at all!*

In your quest to be authentic, it's wise to examine your past and realize how it has affected your self-concept.

Everyone carries around a past with negative experiences. Some of these experiences were our own fault, while others were not. *What's most relevant is how the experiences of the past are interpreted.* It's challenging not to assign meaning to these experiences, but is the meaning that's been assigned accurate? More importantly, is it useful?

There are several signs that you're not using your past constructively:

1. **You continue making the same mistakes.** The past should be useful. From the past, we learn what works and what doesn't, provided the experience is interpreted correctly.

2. **You ignore your past.** Easy to do, but has negative consequences. Time doesn't heal all wounds. Healing heals all wounds. If there's something in your past you feel the desire to forget, it's hurting you in the present.

3. **You've adopted negative attitudes, beliefs, or behavioral characteristics from your parents.** Do you have the same short temper your father had? Do you lie excessively like your mother did? Do you mistrust rich people? Dislike anyone that's a democrat? Beliefs and attitudes that you didn't choose for yourself can be damaging to your self-image.

4. **A single negative experience is affecting your belief system today.** These experiences are most likely to occur in childhood, but aren't limited to your early years.

For example, perhaps you didn't do well in art class in 4th grade.

You may have drawn the conclusion that:

- You have no artistic ability.
- Your art teacher didn't like you.
- Your art teacher wasn't a good teacher.
- You're not a good person because you're not good at creating art.
- You lack any creative ability.
- You're not good at learning new skills.

- You're not very smart.
- You're not a well-rounded person.

And it can snowball from there. Suppose one of your classmates made fun of your drawing in art class.

- I'm not a good enough.
- People don't like me.
- I shouldn't let anyone see something as personal as my artwork in the future.
- I will avoid exposing myself to any criticism in the future by being very reserved and cautious.

It's easy to see how negative and erroneous beliefs can develop from negative experiences. These beliefs can be extremely limiting and influence every part of your life.

"Love yourself first and everything else falls into line. You really have to love yourself to get anything done in this world."

- Lucille Ball

Determine if your past is negatively affecting your self-concept:

1. **Make a list of your beliefs about yourself.** Focus on negative beliefs and any limitations. Include all areas of your life where you feel limited or dissatisfied. A few examples include:

- I'm not good with money.
- No one will hire me.
- I'll never had a good relationship.
- I can't lose weight.
- I don't have any self-control.

2. **Question the belief.** Most of your beliefs aren't justified if you examine them closely. This is an important step.

- Where did this belief come from? Is the source credible?

- Is it based on sufficient evidence? One experience usually isn't enough. Touching a hot stove is sufficient experience to draw a valid conclusion. One failed attempt at dating or starting a business is not.

- Is the belief reasonable?

3. **Determine what the belief is costing you.** Inaccurate beliefs can cause a lot of damage. What are the beliefs you hold about yourself costing you?

- A lack of confidence.
- Lower income.
- Fewer friends or a dissatisfying social life.
- The belief that your options are limited to change your life.
- Overall dissatisfaction with yourself or your life.

4. **Choose an alternate belief.** Choose a belief that better suits reality and supports a healthy self-image. "No one likes me" can become "I am able to make friends easily".

5. **Find evidence.** Staying with the previous example, even if you're friend-free at the moment, you can recall previous friendships. Remember a time in your life when your social life was more active. It's only logical to believe that if you can make a couple of friends, you can also create numerous friendships.

- Convince yourself that your new belief is possible.

It's common to be limited by the past. *We often fail to consider that many of our beliefs about ourselves are based on faulty evidence.* At one point, you didn't walk or read well. Does that mean that you can't do either well today? The human brain feels the need to assign meaning to everything that happens.

Sometimes that meaning is incorrect. Sometimes there is no meaning at all.

Do you have erroneous beliefs that are negatively affecting your self-esteem? In the next phase of this queenly self-concept makeover project, we'll work further on building your self-esteem (it's the one accessory no Queen should ever be without).

Here's what you need to do today:

Review this lessons Affirmations in your course and go through the important process of reevaluating your past by completing the steps below in your journal:

1. Make a list of your negative beliefs about yourself. Then, focus on one belief at a time.
2. Question your belief.
3. Determine what the belief is costing you.
4. Choose an alternate belief.
5. Find evidence of your new belief.

Self-Esteem Like a True Queen

Self-Esteem Like a True Queen

*I*n the last lesson, we looked at how negative experiences in your past can affect your self-concept. Self-esteem isn't quite the same as your self-concept, but they're related.

Your self-concept is your perception of yourself. Your self-esteem is a measure of how happy you are with yourself. By increasing one, you can increase the other. Today, we'll look at building your self-esteem.

It's much easier to present ourselves authentically to others when we feel good about ourselves.

Give your self-esteem a boost and think more highly of yourself:

1. **Guarantee success by starting small.** Success breeds confidence and self-esteem. Create small successes in your life. Drink water instead of soda at lunch. Pay all of your bills on time this month. *Any little thing that would make you feel good about yourself is a great place to start.*

2. **Do something that frightens you.** Afraid of dogs? Make a visit to the dog kennel. Afraid of public speaking? Tell a story to several friends simultaneously. Prove to yourself that you can stretch beyond your current comfort zone.

3. **Show off your strengths.** Are you a great athlete? Sign up for a softball team. Get out and show your stuff. It feels good to do something that you do well. Remind yourself of how skilled and competent you can be. This will boost your confidence and sense of self-esteem. It's enjoyable to show off a little, too.

4. **Do something for others.** When you help someone else, you feel good about yourself. Down deep, the average person worries about being selfish or inconsiderate. Do something for someone else and you'll convince yourself that you're a good person.

5. **Eat a healthier diet.** When you eat poorly, you don't feel good. *You don't know how bad you feel. You're just used to it.* Your mood and outlook on life will improve when you improve your diet.

6. **Avoid comparisons.** There's always someone else smarter, better looking, wealthier, or more charismatic. There are a lot of people in the world. Notice the progress you're making in your life and be happy with that.
   •We always choose exceptional people to compare ourselves to. So

yes, maybe Ariana Grande is better looking, and Oprah Winfrey is wealthier than you. This will always be true for 99.9999% of the population.

7. **Fill your mind with uplifting information.** There are plenty of workshops, music, and books with a positive message. *With positive information entering your brain on a regular basis, you'll be happier with life and yourself.* By the same token, avoid negative information and people.

8. **Observe your thoughts.** If you pay attention to your thoughts, you'll be both amazed and horrified. It's amazing how your mind jumps around to different topics and the crazy things it says. If a real person acted in the same way, you'd call the people in the white coats to come make a pick-up.
   •Notice how odd your self-talk can be.

9. **Create a list of affirmations.** Make a list of affirmations that you'd like to believe and keep it handy. Whenever you mind is idle, repeat your affirmations to yourself. When you're not busy, your mind will start chattering. Take control of the chatter and keep it positive.

10. **Remember your greatness.** You've accomplished some impressive things. Make a list of everything you've managed to do in your life up to this point. It's easy to forget how far you've come. Make a list and review it often.

11. **Learn something new.** Children are so proud of themselves when they learn new something new. It might not be as obvious to us as adults, but we experience the same phenomenon. Learn how to bake a cake from scratch or how to hit a golf ball. What interests you? Try to learn a new skill each month.

12. **Exercise.** You know you're supposed to do it. When you don't do things you know that should be done, you become annoyed with yourself and doubt your self-discipline. Exercise feels good, too. Take care of yourself.

13. **Introduce yourself to someone new.** This activity carries no risk and has a lot of upside. You feel like you have control over your life, begin to eliminate any shyness, and possibly make a new friend. Everyone fears strangers to some extent. Minimize yours and you'll feel more confident and pleased with yourself.

Everyone can benefit from a little more self-esteem. ***When you think more highly of yourself, you're in better position to change your self-concept and your life.*** Think of more ways you can boost your self-esteem and apply these concepts every day.

In the next lesson, you'll see how you can have a more positive self-concept – and raise your self-esteem – by being consciously proactive in several areas of your life.

> **"A healthy self-love means we have no compulsion to justify to ourselves or others why we take vacations, why we sleep late, why we buy new shoes, why we spoil ourselves from time to time. We feel comfortable doing things which add quality and beauty to life."**
> **–Andrew Matthews**

Here's what you need to do today:

1. Complete this lessons affirmations and self-reflection questions in your course.

2. Make one small, positive change to your daily routine starting today. Keep it small and simple.

You'll boost your self-esteem and guarantee your improvement by continuing to perform this small change each day until it becomes a habit.

Increase Your Queenly Satisfaction

❧

*h*erOne of the most reliable ways to enhance your self-concept is to make some positive changes. It's easier to think positively about yourself when you have an enjoyable and successful life.

In this lesson, we continue with our self-concept makeover by looking at how you can take action in several different areas of your life to acquire a more positive self-concept.

There's nothing inherently wrong with living in a studio apartment, eating instant soup every night, and sporting a 45-inch waist. However, happy thoughts are easier to come by when you're pleased with yourself and your life!

Consider the main parts of your life and seek to make the changes you desire.

Health and Well-Being

Are you as healthy and fit as you'd like to be? *It's not necessary to have a 6-pack to show off at the beach, but being healthy has its advantages.* Good health should be a high priority for anyone that values herself. An attractive body also boosts self-esteem and demonstrates to you than you can control yourself.

Prove to yourself that you're worth the time and energy to maintain good health:

1. **See your physician for a checkup.** Everyone should see the doctor at least once per year. There are plenty of health conditions that don't always show obvious symptoms, yet are very serious. Diabetes, hypertension, and high cholesterol are just a few examples.

- Taking care of yourself demonstrates your belief that you're valuable and relevant. An "I don't care" attitude demonstrates the opposite.

2. **Exercise regularly.** Again, show yourself that you're worth the time and energy.

3. **Find and maintain a healthy weight.** No one enjoys being overweight, and it can be a serious challenge to one's self-esteem. However, it's also challenging to change your bodyweight for the better in the long-term.

- *Make small nutritional changes that you can maintain.* Eliminating a can of soda each day and substituting water is one such change.

- Those at a healthy weight simply have better habits. Create healthy habits, one at a time.

Be as healthy as possible. Eat a healthy diet, get some exercise, and see your doctor regularly. ***Take good care of yourself. You're worth it.***

> *"Don't rely on someone else for your happiness and self-worth. Only you can be responsible for that. If you can't love and respect yourself – no one else will be able to make that happen. Accept who you are – completely; the good and the bad – and make changes as YOU see fit – not because you think someone else wants you to be different."*
>
> Stacey Charter

Social Life

No woman (or man) is an island. ***Humans are social creatures, so unless your dream is to sit on top of mountain after taking a vow of silence, it's necessary to involve others in your life.*** Your self-concept is affected by the quality of your social life. If you wish there were more people interested in spending time with you, it's easy to feel bad about yourself.

A more fulfilling social life can be right around the corner:

1. **Decide on the type of social life you desire.** Not everyone wants to be the life of the party and spend time in a large group every night. Maybe you'd rather have a couple of close friends that you meet for dinner once a week and a regular social activity on the weekend. It's up to you. Give it some thought.

2. **Determine what's been standing in your way.** When you know

the cause, you can make a plan. A few possibilities include:

- I work at home and don't have regular contact with others.
- I'm shy.
- I don't know what to say to people.

3. **Create and implement a solution.** There are books on how to be more charismatic. You can find videos on how to get over social anxiety or how to deal with shyness. Maybe you need to reach out to the people you already know. Perhaps you can join a club or start a new hobby that involves other people.

- Build your social life one person at a time. *Most people only need a couple of good friends to feel satisfaction and self-esteem in this part of their lives.*

Building an enjoyable social life is much easier than you think. *Always remember that most people are lonely to varying degrees.* It's not difficult to find others that would like to get out of the house and share a meaningful activity or conversation.

"Don't ask yourself what the world needs, ask yourself what makes you come alive. And then go and do that. Because what the world needs is people who have come alive."

Howard Washington Thurman

Finances

It's hard to be pleased with yourself if you're filling your gas tank $3 at a time. ***Having the ability to pay for life's basic expenses is important to your self-concept.*** It's easy to think negatively about yourself when you can't take care of your expenses.

Get your finances under control:

1. **Create a simple budget and stick to it.** Whether you earn $10,000 or $10 million, everyone needs a budget. There are numerous websites and books dedicated to personal finance and budgeting. Teach yourself what you need to know.

2. **Learn how to save.** A proper budget will provide for an excess of funds at the end of the month. Save it and invest it appropriately.

3. **Earn more.** If you can't meet your expenses with your income, the only solution is to either cut expenses or earn more. There are several ways to increase your income:

- Find a second job.
- Get a raise at your current job.
- Find a better paying job.
- Create a primary or secondary job for yourself. There are many opportunities online in today's world.

Think about the type of financial life that appeals to you and take steps to make it happen. Money isn't everything, but it is relevant. You'll feel more capable and less discouraged if your financial life is healthy.

"You have been criticizing yourself for years, and it hasn't worked.

Try approving of yourself and see what happens."

Louise L. Hay

Have Goals

Do you have goals? ***Being excited about the future and making consistent progress in life will enhance your concept of yourself.*** Numerous studies have shown that those with goals outperform those without goals in every area of life. Having a few goals creates a sense of purpose, direction, and control.

Setting goals is simple and effective:

1. **Set goals with a timeline no longer than 12 weeks.** It's hard to maintain focus and enthusiasm longer than this. If your goal is too big to reach in 12 weeks, set short-term goals that will take you in the right direction.

2. **Measure your progress.** This keeps your goals fresh in your mind and provides the feedback you need to maximize your effectiveness.

3. **Get excited by progress.** If you want to enhance your self-concept, feel good about yourself at every opportunity. Most people have been stuck in the same place for years, so any progress in life is worthy of celebration.

Setting goals can be a complicated process, but it doesn't have to be. ***Having a few goals and making regular progress can be great for your self-concept.*** It proves to you that you can make changes in your life and control your future.

Give of Yourself Regularly

It's not all about you. Your self-concept isn't all about you either. *It's also about your perception of your value to the world.* Providing value to the world selflessly is a great way to change your self-concept and boost your self-esteem.

1. **Volunteer.** Organizations are always looking for more volunteers. Find something that appeals to you and get involved.

2. **Find a job or second job that helps others.** You could tutor children or teach adults to read. Maybe you work with senior citizens one night a week in the evenings. There are many jobs available that provide a meaningful service to others.

3. **Random acts of kindness.** Life presents endless opportunities to help others. You can't help but love yourself when you're doing something wonderful for another person.

Help others when possible and you'll benefit in many unpredictable ways. Think about your average day. What small changes could you make to be more helpful or kind to others?

You have a higher opinion of yourself when you're pleased in these main areas of your life. *The more satisfied you are with yourself, the easier it is to be authentic.*

Your next lesson finishes your makeover with giving you some prompts to help you reflect on others you look up to. They may be great examples for you to follow when deciding what kind of action you may want to take to bring more satisfaction to your life.

Here's what you need to do today:

Complete this lessons affirmation and set a 12-week goal to make one change in one of the areas mentioned in this lesson. Make the goal small enough that you'll find it pretty easy to see success with it.

Write down your goal and remind yourself of your new goal several times each day. But avoid just *thinking* about it – take action each day to make it happen.

What Kind of Queen Do You Wish To Be?

*T*his last lesson in your queenly self-concept makeover gives you one more way to enhance your self-concept and self-esteem. When we see concrete examples of the qualities we admire, it can inspire us to do the same.

Most of us never aspired to be an average person working in a cubicle at a job we don't enjoy. ***When you can be the person you've always wanted to be, your self-concept will be perfect for you.*** Isn't this what everyone dreams about? When you're the person you want to be, you'll have the life you desire.

Consciously decide who you want to be:

1. **Who do you admire and why?** Do you wish you were more like Wonder Woman? Why? Are you a fan of Michelle Obama? Marie Curie? Why?

2. **What personal qualities have you always admired in others?**

- Charisma?
- Confidence?
- Mental toughness?
- Kindness?
- Cool under pressure?
- Happiness?

3. **What can you do today to start being the person you've always wanted to be?** There's no one that can stop you. Anyone that tries to get in your way can be ignored. Be on a mission to become the person you would admire.

This is the ultimate goal. *If you're the person (ahem... queen) you wish to be and living the life you desire, your opinion of yourself will be at the highest possible level.* Everything else is just a steppingstone to reach this point.

Even as you work on enhancing your queenly self-concept, it's important to accept yourself, wherever you may be on your journey. We'll pause for summary and reflection of this self-concept makeover in the next lesson. Then, the next module guides you through the process of accepting who you are.

"Because one believes in oneself, one doesn't try to convince others. Because one is content with oneself, one doesn't need others' approval. Because one accepts oneself, the whole world accepts him or her

Lao-Tzu

Here's what you need to do today:

In your journal, write down one quality that you admire in someone else. How can you start demonstrating this quality yourself?

Make a note to remind yourself to practice it each day.

Now let's get logged into the course to complete this lesson's affirmation and self-reflection: Each Day I Strive To Become The Person I Want To Be

Reflecting on Dragons

Queen, your self-concept has been shaped by your past. Or rather, your perception of your past. **Review the uncomfortable experiences a.k.a dragons from your past and find a more positive resolution.** Remember that the past is over and no indication of what the future can hold. The past is only a limitation if you allow it to be.

Building your self-esteem will give you the fuel to make alterations to your self-concept. This is an ongoing process. You already have plenty of reasons to be happy with yourself. Ensure you remind yourself of how wonderful you already are.

Be proactive about enhancing your life and kingdom according to your own wishes. By creating and living the life you desire, your self-concept will change. When you have evidence that you're living your idea of a happy life, you've achieved the ultimate.

You can be authentic and proud to present yourself to the world just the way you are!

Self-Reflection Questions:

What are the limiting beliefs I hold that were created through past experiences?

Are these limiting beliefs valid? Where did they come from? Is it possible I interpreted the situation incorrectly?

How is my current life limiting my beliefs about myself, my capabilities, and my ability to control my future and my environment?

What changes do I need to make to my finances, health, and social life to support a more effective self-concept?

Who do I want to become? Who do I admire?

What can I do today to begin living more like the person I want to be?

How would I rate my self-esteem? What are the biggest barriers to feeling better about myself and what can I do to overcome those barriers?

In the next part of your journey, you'll discover strategies to help you slay even more dragons: overcoming barriers to accepting yourself and building a positive, healthy, and queenly self-image.

Queenly Self-Concept Quiz

❧❦❧

Choose the correct answers.

1. Is it possible that some of the things you believe about yourself aren't true at all?

- a. Yes
- b. No

2. What is the most relevant item to your self-concept?

- a. The truth about the experiences of your past
- b. What TV shows you watched as a kid
- c. Your dreams when you're asleep
- d. How you interpret the experiences of your past

3. Ignoring your past is the most constructive way to use it.

- a. True
- b. False

4. It's easier to present yourself authentically to others when you can:

- a. Feel good about yourself
- b. Hide your past
- c. Eat as much as you want
- d. All of the above

5. Which strategies will build your self-esteem?

- a. Show off your strengths
- b. Do something for others
- c. Learn something new
- d. All of the above

6. Which situation is more likely to inspire you to change your life?

- a. When you think more highly of yourself
- b. When you think you're a failure, so you should change
- c. Watching an entertaining TV show
- d. All of the above

7. One of the more reliable ways to enhance your self-concept is to:

- a. Watch TV
- b. Make some positive changes
- c. Take a nap
- d. Cheat at a contest to ensure that you'll be the winner

8. Exercising regularly can raise your self-concept.

- a. True
- b. False

9. Setting goals within this timeline is usually the most effective for maintaining focus and enthusiasm:

- a. 10 years
- b. 1 year
- c. 6 months
- d. 12 weeks

10. If you have a healthy self-concept, you shouldn't aspire for more than you have.

- a. True
- b. False

III

Accepting The Queen Within

An important part of authenticity is accepting yourself. In the process of accepting yourself, it's important to forgive yourself for your past mistakes and develop a positive self-image so you can move forward toward creating a life that you'll enjoy.

Queenly Acceptance

What It Is and How To Get It

*I*n order to live authentically, it's important to accept who you are. You want to feel comfortable showing yourself to the world. So far, we've gone through the process of knowing yourself and giving yourself a self-concept makeover. This module will help you accept yourself just the way you are.

Accepting yourself is also the first step to building self-esteem. ***It's not possible to feel positive about yourself if you can't accept yourself.*** Self-acceptance is the level of happiness and satisfaction you have with yourself.

Many mental health professionals believe that self-acceptance is necessary before change can occur. If you're feeling stuck, a lack of self-acceptance may be the first challenge to overcome. Accepting your flaws allows you to change them.

Learn to accept yourself and enjoy the person you are:

1. **Let go of your parents' behavior.** Some parents are better than others. Overly critical parents don't have bad children, they're just lousy parents. There's little to be gained by giving your parents a hard time for their inadequacies. The solution is to forgive them and release yourself from the past.

  • Avoid judging yourself based on the parenting you received. *It's a reflection of them, not you.*

2. **Volunteer.** There's no easier way to convince yourself that you're worthy of self-acceptance than to volunteer your time with someone that needs you. *Prove to yourself how great a person you are.* There are countless opportunities to volunteer in your community.

3. **Be proud of your strengths.** It's hard to accept yourself if you're constantly reminding yourself of your weaknesses. Make a long list that you can return to in the future. List every positive thing you can about yourself. *Even the smallest positive attribute is worthy of mention.*

  • *"I am a good person."*
  • *"I can play the banjo."*
  • *"I am loyal to my friends."*

4. **Forgive yourself.** If you're harping on your past transgressions, self-acceptance will be in short-supply. Chalk your bad choices up to

experience and move on.

- Everyone does the best they can. There will always be moments where you're less capable than others. You can do better next time.

5. **Let go of goals that will never be reached.** If you're 57 years old, your childhood dream of becoming an astronaut is over. It is. It's difficult to accept yourself when the life you're living is very different from your original plans. There's a time to let it all go. Let the present moment be that time. *Make new plans that are plausible and that excite you.*

6. **Eliminate negative self-talk.** You can't accept yourself if you're constantly insulting yourself. *Give yourself a fighting chance* to reach a state of self-acceptance. Speak to yourself the way you would a good friend. Be a friend to yourself.

7. **Be authentic.** When you put on a persona for the world, you're not giving others the opportunity to accept you as you are. How will you be able to accept yourself? When you're authentic, the love you receive feels infinitely more meaningful. Living honestly is scary, but surprisingly easy. People admire and respect those with the strength to be authentic.

8. **Recognize your worth to the world.** Fortunately, this isn't something that must be earned. You're born with it. How much could you contribute if you applied yourself? *The world needs you.* What could say more of your inherent value than the fact that the world needs you?

9. **Forgive others.** The ability to forgive others is proportional to your ability to forgive yourself. Practice forgiving others and you'll find self-acceptance comes much easier.

Self-acceptance is fancy word for tolerating yourself. No one is perfect. You accept your friends and family even though they're all flawed in a unique way. Give yourself the same latitude. *Focus on your positive traits and forgive yourself for your flaws and mistakes.* Accept yourself as you are and you'll find that as you live authentically, others will be more accepting as well.

Accepting yourself can be a hard proposition, so the next few lessons will take you through several strategies that help you get through the main pitfalls you're likely to encounter in this part of your journey to authenticity. You'll learn to forgive yourself and let go of past mistakes, break free of crippling self-doubts, and build a healthy self-image you can be proud of.

First, in your next lesson, you'll find four ways that help you to come to terms with your true self.

Here's what you need to do today:

Be proud of your strengths! In your journal, write down every positive thing about you that you can think of. Reflect on how wonderful you are!

After that's done login to the course and complete this lesson's Affirmation and Self Reflection Questions.

The Queen Inside

***

4 Ways to Come to Terms with the Queen in the Mirror.

*E*ven as you're learning to accept yourself, there will likely be times when you're unhappy with who you are, what you've attained in life, or which path you're taking. That's because you're human. *Those sentiments affect all of us from time to time.* Sure, there will be days when your best doesn't seem good enough to you, but what if your best is really just fine?

Coming to terms with your true self can help you acknowledge the awesome person you really are. Your various characteristics combine to make something totally unique and special. No one else has your individual talents. No one else could ever take your unique place in this world.

Accepting yourself for who you truly are can also boost your confidence and help you take advantage of your innate skills for your own benefit and that of others as well.

Try these strategies to achieve contentment with the skin you're in:

1. **Know that you are special.** It's important that you look at the person you are as a beautiful creation. ***You weren't made this way by mistake.*** Your beliefs, likes, and dislikes are all part of a magnificent design.

2. **Look at the bright side.** Often times, you probably feel that someone else's situation is better than yours because they have more, seem to be happier, or appear better off than you. But if you take a moment to look at the circumstances of others who are "less blessed" than you are, you'll realize that there is actually a bright side to your life.

- Do you know anyone who couldn't find work for so long that they've given up on it?
- Is there anyone around you who's suffering the pain of losing a loved one?
- When was the last time you noticed how many homeless people live under the freeway?

3. **Consider your accomplishments.** Throughout your life, you've probably achieved lots of things, both personally and professionally. Whether you accomplished a stronger bond with your parents, or completion of a project that won your workplace a new contract, those things all took place while you were in the skin you're in today.

- Remember that the person who has those accomplishments is the *true you* – you did it with your own strength, abilities and sensibilities.

- ***You're a winner in your own right*** by merit of what you've accomplished, and no one can take those victories away from you.

4. **Avoid underestimating yourself.** One important factor that may be causing you to feel less than happy with who you are and where you are in life is the fact that you may be underestimating yourself. It's possible that you don't have what you want because you haven't really tried to get it!

- Instead of wishing you had what somebody else has, why not put some thought into how you can achieve it for yourself? ***Make a detailed plan of achievable steps to get what you want.***

- Stop and consider that there's really nothing separating you from your goals because you have what it takes to work towards it.

You were uniquely created with the talents and skills to have a fulfilling life, not a life of regrets! Your next lesson will show you three strategies to help you let go of your past mistakes and move forward.

Here's what you need to do today:

Write down in your journal one thing that you are dissatisfied with in your life.

Reflect on what the silver lining for this situation could be.

Write a detailed plan for how you could change this situation for the better.

Complete this lesson's affirmation and reflection in your online course.

Slay Old Dragons and Move Forward

⁓◈◈◈⁓

*I*n the last two lessons, we looked at some strategies for self-acceptance like a true queen. Often, one reason why self-acceptance is so hard is that the most difficult person for us to forgive is usually ourselves. Regret, shame, and guilt prevent us from letting go of our past mistakes.

Rather than reflecting on the experience and learning from it so that we can move forward, we tend to dwell on these unfortunate times.

By refusing to forgive ourselves of our regrets, we remain trapped in the past.

The good news is that there are some simple strategies that can help you come to terms with the things that you have done in the past, learn from these missteps, and embrace a future that includes a fulfilling life.

Try these strategies to help you forgive yourself and move forward:

1. Be honest with yourself and others about your error and hold yourself accountable. Reflect on the mistake that you're unable to get over. Clearly identify what you did or didn't do and own up to it instead of trying to justify your actions.

- *Being honest with yourself and stating where you went wrong is the first step to releasing the pain, guilt, and shame that you feel.*

- Examine the events and circumstances that led to your faux pas and be honest about how you felt then and are feeling now.

- Consider how your mistake impacted others in both a physical and emotional sense.

- Talk about your slip-up with a close friend, relative, counselor, or religious leader that you trust. Seek their opinion, feedback, and guidance about the severity of your error. It's likely that they'll see your mistake in a more forgiving light than you do.

2. **Try to remedy the situation and make amends.** Consider what you could have done differently to prevent your misstep and *develop a plan to act differently if you face a similar situation in the future.* This can help you forgive yourself.

- Even if it has been quite some time since the situation occurred, if the result of your blunder caused harm to others, consider offering an apology and asking for forgiveness. This action alone can be very healing for both you and the person that suffered harm as a result of your mistake.

- If you're unable to make amends with those who were directly affected, consider doing good deeds and acts of kindness to show to yourself and others that you truly regret your actions.

- ***If your poor decision resulted in a monetary loss, seek to make restitution.***

- Share your story with others so that they might be able to avoid making the same error.

3. **Realize that you've grown and you're no longer the same person that made the original slip-up.** Continue to seek ways to help others and avoid actions that might lead to a similar lapse of judgment in the future.

All of us make mistakes, and sometimes they come with serious and grave consequences. Regardless of how serious our errors might have been, all of us deserve forgiveness. The next lesson will show you how to forgive yourself.

Here's what you need to do today:

Start with one mistake that you would like to let go of. Follow the suggested process:

1. Hold yourself accountable for the error.

2. Try to remedy the situation and make amends.
3. Realize that you've grown and changed since you made the mistake and remind yourself that similar situations will not lead you to make the same mistake again.

Complete your affirmations and self-reflections for this lesson in the Prince, Not Required online course:

- Free Yourself From The Past
- I Forgive Myself For Any And All Past Mistakes

Drop the Mantle of Guilt and Pick up the Scepter of Joy

❧

*I*n the last lesson, you learned how to let go of your mistakes and slay old dragons. But sometimes, the guilt still remains. Only sociopaths are able to completely avoid guilt. ***Feelings of guilt are distressing and draining.*** What can be done about it now?

Get over your guilt with these strategies:

1. **Determine if you should feel guilty.** Whose standards are you using? Your parents'? Your own? Your church's? Can you be sure the source is correct? Ensure that you're judging yourself by a set of standards you deem to be worthy. It's your choice.

2. **Learn from it.** Why do you feel guilty? Obviously, you did or said something that you consider to be wrong. Once you know why you feel guilty, you're in a position to benefit from it. ***Ensure that you don't repeat the behavior in the future.***

- Visualize yourself behaving in a new and improved manner.

3. **Sometimes guilt is unproductive.** Imagine that you feel guilty about missing your child's play because you were required to work. If you did everything within your power, there's no benefit to feeling guilt. *Does your behavior require modification? If not, there's no reason to feel guilty.*

4. **Apologize.** It can be as simple as saying you're sorry. You'll feel better afterwards, even if your apology is rejected.

5. **Accept that you feel guilty.** Acknowledge your feelings and the pain that goes with them. Accept that you made a mistake. Realize that it will pass.

6. **Forgive yourself.** Even if the other person won't forgive you, you can forgive yourself. Be kind and gentle with yourself. No one is perfect.

7. **Let it go.** Once the event is over, you've apologized, and modified your behavior, let it go. At that point, what purpose does your guilt serve? Take a deep breath, let it out, and move on. *Keep your mind occupied with more productive thoughts.*

8. **Have gratitude.** Rather than saying to yourself, *"I should have told Mary the truth"*, tell yourself, *"I'm grateful I've learned the importance of honesty."* Negative experiences can still be worthy of gratitude.

Avoid guilt in the future:

1. **Think instead of react.** Guilt is often the result of acting without thinking. ***When you become emotional, take a moment to collect yourself.*** It's easy to do or say something that you'll later regret.

2. **Be less critical of yourself.** Guilt and the need to be perfect go hand in hand. ***Avoid expecting perfection.*** It's unrealistic and leads to feelings of guilt. Everyone makes mistakes on a daily basis.

3. **Create realistic beliefs.** Maybe you believe that a good parent should do certain things, but you don't or can't do them. Are you sure your opinion on the matter is reasonable? Maybe you believe that a good parent would never get frustrated, which is unrealistic.

You're not alone in feeling guilty. Some people spend a lifetime wallowing in guilt. ***How long you feel guilty is up to you.*** Learn from your mistakes and go forward with a new perspective and strategy. Apologize and forgive yourself.

The real shame is repeating behavior that results in guilt. Avoid repeating your mistakes and be gentle with yourself. ***Practice making the choice that doesn't result in guilt.*** The more you practice, the more healthy choices you'll make, and the less guilt you'll have to deal with.

Still having trouble forgiving yourself?

Consider this 4-step process:

The 4 Most Important Steps to Forgiving Yourself

Sometimes, it's difficult to forgive your own missteps. You feel really rotten when you've let yourself or someone else down. But one day, you have to allow the sun to shine again. Has it been challenging to do that?

This 4-step process can help you forgive yourself and move on with your life:

1. **Confront your mistake.** In all circumstances, take responsibility for your error. Come face to face with it and acknowledge where you stumbled. As painful as it might be, this is the first step to forgiving yourself.

- It's sometimes helpful to look in the mirror and say aloud what you did. It connects you with the action. ***It also helps you realize that it's okay to make mistakes.***

- Therapy can help if the first option doesn't do the trick. Talking to someone else may help you release feelings that are tied down inside.

2. **Analyze the impact.** ***Take a moment to reflect on the outcome of your actions.*** Who has been affected? How badly were you or others hurt? Take it all at face value, and avoid embellishing it with undeserved emotion.

- Take the time to consider the impact outside of what you initially see. It's sometimes easy to overlook the smaller impact when the greater one is overwhelming.

3. **Accept your human imperfections.** Above all, be kind to yourself. Remind yourself that you're human. There's nobody on the face of the earth who goes through life without making mistakes. However, it's important to remember that this doesn't excuse what happened.

- While accepting your human imperfections, take the time to identify your shortcomings. Use the opportunity to work on aspects of yourself that you might want to improve. Perhaps you'd like to further develop certain character traits or strengthen your skills in particular areas.

- When apologizing to yourself and others, you can point out that everybody makes mistakes, but you've learned from yours and have every intention of not repeating it.

4. **Challenge yourself to do better.** *The crucial final step to self-forgiveness is challenging yourself to do better.* In the previous step, you accepted your imperfections. Now it's time to work at fixing the things you can.

- Is it that you need to learn to be nicer to others? You can work on that through conscious effort or group therapy.

- Try not to repeat the same mistake. That's one of the easiest ways to backslide and end up at square one again.

- Ask your supportive friends and family to help you on your journey. Remember that no man is an island.

Making things right might not happen overnight. ***What's important is that you forgive yourself and commit to turning things around.***

You're full of so much potential. That potential sits unused while you consume yourself with negative energy. Lift yourself up! Come to terms with the fact that you have so much more to give to the world. Chip away at the negativity until all that's left is your renewed spirit.

The next lesson will help you chip away at that negativity as you leave your inner critic behind!

Here's what you need to do today:

Complete this lesson's affirmation and self-reflection. In your journal, write down a mistake that you're having trouble forgiving yourself for. Follow this process:

1. Confront your mistake.
2. Analyze the impact
3. Accept your human imperfection
4. Vow that you won't make the same mistake again. Take action to ensure a more positive outcome in similar situations.

Transform Your Inner Frog Into Your Own Personal Princess

~~~

In the past few lessons, we learned about self-acceptance, slaying inner dragons to let go of your mistakes, and forgiving yourself for those mistakes. But what about your faults?

It's easy to beat yourself up over your shortcomings and failures. *Your inner critic (frog) is attempting to protect you, but like an overprotective parent, it's causing more harm than good.* Criticizing yourself only serves to make life more challenging. It also robs you of options and puts limits on your life.

Your inner critic provides information, but that doesn't mean you have to listen. Your inner critic is relentless. It's active from the moment you wake up until you fall asleep. It's even active in your dreams! Your inner critic won't be contained easily.

Change what your inner critic says to you and reach your full potential:

1. **Drown it out.** Fill your mind with positive talk and imagery. Avoid giving your inner critic any room to make its opinions known to you. Keep your self-talk positive and expect the best to happen.

2. **Recognize the truth.** *Your inner critic is just a manifestation of your fear.* Its sole purpose is to stop you from harming yourself. However, it's like a scared child. You tell yourself that you're an idiot or that you can't do something in order to have an excuse not to expose yourself to failure.

   • Your inner critic is the villain. Consider treating it as such.

3. **Empty your mind.** If you need to make a phone call or finish your taxes, keep your mind empty and get started. It's your thoughts that stop you from getting things done. Keep your mind clear and get busy. *Action is the best way to keep your critic at bay.*

4. **It's all a matter of moving your hands or moving your mouth.** Consider every action at your disposal. They're all a matter of either doing something or saying something. That's all there is to life. You're either physically doing something or talking.

   • There's no practical difference between calling your best friend and making a cold call. You're dialing the phone with your hands and speaking with your mouth.

   • How can an inner critic exist when every action you take is either moving your hands or your mouth? It's all the same.

5. **What would you tell a friend?** Would you judge a friend as harshly as you judge yourself? What would you say to them in a similar situation? What would you say to your child? There's no reason not to treat yourself just as kindly. *Be a friend to yourself.*

6. **Say something encouraging to yourself every 10 minutes.** Set a timer on your phone or computer. Get in the habit of encouraging yourself each day. After 18 hours, you will have said 108 positive things to yourself. It won't take long to create a new habit at that pace. *Criticizing yourself is a habit. Encouraging yourself is also a habit.*

7. **Make a list of your high points.** Think about your greatest successes. It's easy to fixate on a few bad choices but choose to focus on your highest achievements. Make a long list and review it regularly. You'll enhance your mood and put your critic to bed.

The inner critic in your head limits your life and your opportunities. Remember that your inner critic is no different from a child afraid of the dark. It isn't rational. You don't have to listen.

Take control of your inner talk and lift yourself up. Speak to yourself the way you would a good friend or loved one. Turn your inner critic into your most positive supporter and you'll live a life you enjoy.

In the next lesson, we'll look at how to break free from crippling self-doubts.

Here's what you need to do today:

Login in to your course and complete 12 Signs That You're Being Too Self-Critical.

For the rest of the day, say something encouraging to yourself every 10 minutes. Every time you start to have a criticizing thought, drown it out with something positive.

Break Free From the Crippling Curse of Self-Doubt

❦

As you continue on your Queen's journey to self-acceptance, it's important to learn how to get past your doubts. These doubts can destroy your confidence and make you feel like you're less than you really are.

Poor self-esteem and a lack of self-confidence can be just as damaging to our lives as being overconfident or arrogant. Do you harbor insecurities about your true abilities and worth? If so, **this doubt is holding you back from reaching your full potential.**

Luckily, you don't have to let fear keep you from achieving your dreams and ambitions in life. There are steps you can take that will help you build your confidence, face your fears, and become free of self-doubt.

Try these tips to erase your self-doubt, gain confidence, and succeed:

1. **Reflect on your past success.** It's natural to feel a bit nervous if you've just been given a new task or responsibility. If you start to doubt your abilities, reflect on your past achievements and feel confident that your prior successes will carry over into this new area.

- Even if you have some lingering doubts, be confident with the knowledge that you wouldn't be in this new position if others didn't think you were up to the challenge.

- *Seeking additional skill training in an area that matches or compliments your new duties can give you confidence in your new role.*

- Be willing to ask others for advice and guidance as you adjust to your new role. Their feedback can help you increase your skills and boost your self-esteem.

2. **Learn to change your negative self-talk into positive affirmations.** Our brains are constantly working to fulfill our inner thoughts and beliefs. When you're overwhelmed with self-doubt, chances are that you're subconsciously listening to negative self-talk from your brain.

- Take control of your inner voice and turn a negative into a positive by replacing your doubts with positive affirmations!

- Rather than focusing on your limitations, *focus on what you can do.* Capitalize on your strengths and write out 10 statements that affirm who you are at the core of your being. Then record how your strength and abilities will help you achieve your task or goal.

- Start each day by repeating your daily affirmations. Then, repeat them whenever you start to worry or feel self-doubt.

3. **Gain perspective by finding cheerleaders, mentors, and other guides.** Do you have a difficult time maintaining a positive sense of self-worth? *It's critical that you take time to connect and build relationships with those that build you up, rather than tear you down.*

- Seek out mentors for your personal and professional life that can give you an unbiased opinion on what you're doing well in various areas. They can also provide insight on what you could change to move forward.

- Build relationships with friends and family members that encourage and rejuvenate you with their positive energy. Minimize contact with those who are overly critical, jealous, or negative. They just drain your energy and bring you down.

- *By surrounding yourself with positive individuals, you'll receive the boost of energy and confidence you need to power through your moments of self-doubt.* You'll then begin to achieve your goals and dreams, rather than holding yourself back!

Everyone faces self-doubt and insecurities from time to time. Practicing these tips can help you defeat self-doubt.

The mistakes of the past, along with damaged self-esteem caused by doubts and fears, may have led to a negative self-image. So let's see how to overcome this negativity as well. Your next lesson gives you nine proven strategies to eliminate a negative self-image.

Here's what you need to do today:

Take control of your inner voice and turn a negative into a positive by replacing your doubts with positive affirmations. In your journal, write a few short, positive affirmations that you can practice to overcome your doubts.

For the rest of the day, each time you doubt yourself, immediately replace that doubt with a positive affirmation. Start with the one's for this lesson available in your Prince, Not Required course.

Defeat the Negative Self-Image Dragon

$\sim\!\!\!\text{∽◔◑◔∽}\!\!\!\sim$

*S*o far in this self-acceptance module, you've learned strategies that can help you accept yourself as you forgive yourself for past mistakes, leave your inner critic behind, and break free from crippling self-doubts. These negative situations, though, may have left their mark on your self-image.

Your self-image is your perception of yourself. You might think of yourself as intelligent, lazy, bad with money, likable, and eccentric. ***Your beliefs about yourself can be liberating or constricting.***

Your self-image can influence your decisions and limit your ability to succeed. For example, if you believe that you're bad at speaking with strangers, you may avoid social situations that include people you don't know. As a result, you might miss out on your biggest opportunity to meet the love of your life, a recruiter for your dream job, or a life-long friend.

Change your self-image and enhance your life with these techniques:

1. **Address your bad habits.** No one is perfect. If you're being completely honest, there are things about you that could use a little work. Shore up your shortcomings. Get in shape, practice being more patient, or be a better friend.

   • *Focus on making progress.* Perfection is an unreasonable goal.

2. **Make a list of your good points.** Do this in the morning and the evening. Make a long list and then add at least one item each morning and evening. Remind yourself of all the things you're already good at. What do you appreciate about yourself? Review the list regularly and notice how good you feel.

3. **Live by your morals.** You have your own opinion about what's right and wrong. If you can live according to your values, how can you feel bad about yourself? *It's only when we stray that we feel guilty or displeased with ourselves.*

   • Make a list of the behaviors you'll no longer accept from yourself.

   • How do you think a person should behave? What qualities are most important to you? Set standards for yourself that you refuse to violate.

4. **Spend time each week helping others.** Volunteer or help a neighbor. Do something for someone else without receiving anything

in return. ***Your self-image will improve considerably by this one strategy alone.***

- There are websites that list the volunteer opportunities in every city. Find your community's listings and make a positive difference in someone's life. You'll benefit as much as they do.

5. **Experience success.** ***You have the right to feel good about any success, so make it easy to succeed.*** Set small goals and accomplish them. It could be a goal to save $100 this month or make it to the gym three times this week. Show yourself that you can be successful consistently.

6. **Spend time with those that think highly of you.** A great way to increase your respect for yourself is to spend time with others who already think you're great. Avoid those that are negative, unkind, or unsupportive.

7. **Spend time on activities that you enjoy.** Make yourself feel good on a regular basis. You can carry those good feelings with you into other parts of your life. ***The more time you're able to spend feeling positive emotions, the better you'll feel about yourself.***

8. **Let go of the need to be perfect.** If being perfect is the only way you can feel good about yourself, you're going to be unhappy most of the time. Perfection isn't possible. Be interested in improvement and effort. These are controllable and achievable.

9. **Treat yourself well.** By treating yourself well, you'll believe that you deserve it. Be as kind to yourself as you would a good friend. Take care of your needs. This includes eating well, getting enough

sleep, having an active social life, and buying yourself the things you need.

Do you think highly of yourself?

A negative self-image can have negative repercussions on every part of your life. It's well worth the time to enhance your self-image. You'll find it difficult to achieve more than you think you deserve. So believe that you deserve a lot and you'll enjoy more of what you desire in life.

We'll end this self-acceptance part of your journey to authenticity in the next lesson as you learn to build a healthy self-image you can be proud of!

Here's what you need to do today:

Spend time with those that think highly of you. Call your most positive friend or loved one and schedule time for coffee, tea, or drinks together.

After that log in to your course and learn how: Affirmative Self Talk Gets In The Way Of Negative Energy.

Building a Queenly Self-Image

*P*reviously in your journey to Accepting the Queen Within, you've learned a lot about overcoming things that can negatively affect what you think of yourself. Today, we finish the self-acceptance part of the course with strategies to help you build up yourself with a positive and healthy self-image.

Reaching your full potential is dependent on the creation and maintenance of a healthy self-image. ***It's not possible to be highly successful if you don't believe in yourself.*** The way you view yourself is either uplifting or a hindrance. Regardless of your childhood experiences, past failings, or current level of self-esteem, you can possess a healthy self-image.

Avoid underestimating the impact of your self-image on other areas of your life. To reach your full potential, you must respect yourself and believe you can do great things.

Prince, Not Required

Add value to yourself, and your self-image will flourish:

1. **Overcome any limiting beliefs.** Think about something you'd like to accomplish but are unable to do because of a limiting belief. Make a list of how that belief is negatively impacting your life. Now, focus on how much your life would be enhanced if you were able to remove this belief from your life.

   • Create five affirmations you can repeat to yourself throughout the day. The affirmations should be stated in the positive and address the new belief you'd like to install.

2. **Recognize the small victories.** It's not necessary to earn a million dollars or lose 50 pounds before you have the right to feel proud and excited. Any progress is worthy of recognizing. *Large successes are the culmination of many smaller successes.*

3. **Take full responsibility for your current situation.** Is it your fault that your parents mistreated you or that your boss is a jerk? Of course not, but no one else is going to fix the situation. It's all on you. *When you take responsibility, you have control.* Self-esteem is elusive when you believe you don't have control over your life.

4. **Do something for others.** It's easy to feel selfish when all of your thoughts and activities are centered on yourself. Spend part of your time enhancing the lives of others. Demonstrate to yourself that you're a good person.

5. **Take a step each day toward your ideal self.** We all have a vision of the person we'd like to be. That ideal version of ourselves

102

might seem too far away to even consider, but take a small step each day. Each small improvement will raise your self-image. Start today by listing all the qualities you'd like to have.

6. **Manage your self-talk.** We all talk to ourselves. You're not the only one! *The greatest thing about this is that we can control what we say to ourselves.* Is your self-talk positive or negative? Negative self-talk chips away at your feelings of self-worth. Be kind to yourself. Be encouraging, positive, and patient.

7. **Get started on the bigger projects in your life.** Your self-image is damaged when you fail to control yourself. Big projects are intimidating. Focus on getting started. Take at least a few minutes each day to tackle the bigger goals in your life. *Sustained progress is the key.*

8. **Avoid comparing yourself to others.** We all have different skills and talents. It's unfair to compare yourself to other people. You're doomed to be either too hard or too easy on yourself.

- Compare yourself to your past. Are you doing better than you were last month? When you can consistently answer "yes," you'll be well on your way to maximizing your self-image.

Begin to build a healthy self-image today. *Regardless of your past or current impressions of yourself, you can learn to view yourself in a more positive light.* A healthy self-image is the springboard to happiness and success. Focus on the small victories in your life and be proud of your progress. You deserve to be successful and happy.

In your next lesson, we pause for summary and reflection of this queenly self-acceptance module. Then, you can surpass simple acceptance by learning how to love yourself!

Here's what you need to do today:

Login to your course and focus on the takeaway: Being Different Makes Me Interesting.

Then, do something for others: Schedule a time this week that you can use for helping someone else. You may want to volunteer at a charity event, help someone you love, or lend a helping hand to someone in need, like taking clothes, blankets, or food to a family experiencing hard times.

Whatever you decide, have a happy heart and devote your full energies to helping out while you're involved in your project.

Focusing On Your Queenly Reflection

*I*n order to live with queenly authenticity, it's important that you know yourself and accept the person you are – flaws and strengths both. Since you've already discovered all about you, this module takes you through several steps to help you gain self-acceptance.

You can help yourself let go of your past mistakes by analyzing the situations in which you made errors. Take responsibility for your mistakes, make amends where you can, and remember that you've learned and grown since then. Forgiving yourself for these mistakes is most important, so you can finally let go of them and move on.

One reason why it's often hard to accept yourself is because of the voice inside you that tells you, "You're not good enough." However, it's possible to completely change your self-talk to say positive things instead of negative. Imagine how uplifting it can be when your self-talk encourages you all day long!

Even with an encouraging voice, you may still be plagued with doubts. Learn how to get rid of these doubts and any lingering issues that cause you to have a negative self-image.

Lastly, you discover techniques that help you build a healthy, positive self-image. Not only will you be happier with yourself, but you'll also move further along the path to being able to live authentically. You'll be proud to show the world who you really are!

Self-Reflection Questions:

How can accepting myself help me live authentically?

What parts of my personality do I have trouble accepting? Why is that?

Are any of my past mistakes keeping me from living the life I desire? What do I need to do to make amends for these mistakes and move on from them?

What does my self-talk say to me throughout most of each day?

How can I make my self-talk say more of the things I'd like to hear?

What types of situations cause me to doubt myself? How can I practice being more self-confident in these situations?

How would I describe my self-image? What can I do to make my self-image more positive?

Now that you have a queenly and healthy self-image, in part four, you'll discover how to move past acceptance and actually love the queen you are. Get a head start by completing this lesson online affirmation: I Accept Myself Wholly And Completely.

Accepting the Queen Within Quiz

*C*hoose the correct answers.

1. What is the first step to building self-esteem?

- a. Focusing on your faults
- b. Accepting yourself
- c. Watching TV
- d. Having the nicest house in the neighborhood

2. Which activity can help you build your self-esteem?

- a. Volunteering your time
- b. Forgiving someone else for what they did to you
- c. Eliminating negative self-talk
- d. All of the above

3. One important factor that may be causing you to feel less than

happy with who you are and where you are in life is the fact that you may be underestimating yourself.

- a. True
- b. False

4. Which of the following strategies will help you let go of a past mistake and move on?

- a. Trying to forget it
- b. Hiding it from others
- c. Holding yourself accountable for the mistake
- d. Blaming the error on someone else

5. Who is able to completely avoid guilt?

- a. Sociopaths
- b. Everyone, if they know the right techniques
- c. Introverts
- d. All of the above

6. The inner critic in your head limits your life and your opportunities.

- a. True
- b. False

7. Which of these strategies will help silence your inner critic?

- a. Reflecting on your past successes
- b. Learning to change negative self-talk into positive affirmations
- c. Finding friends with positive attitudes
- d. All of the above

8. What is your self-image?

- a. What your dog thinks about you
- b. Your idea of what you think you should be like
- c. Your perception of yourself
- d. A character in your favorite TV show

9. Which strategy is more likely to help you eliminate a negative self-image?

- a. Eating ice cream
- b. Spending time on activities that you enjoy
- c. Watching TV
- d. All of the above

10. Regardless of your childhood experiences, past failings, or current level of self-esteem, you can possess a healthy self-image.

- a. True
- b. False

IV

Wearing Your Self-Love Crown Proudly

In this module, you'll move past acceptance and learn how to actually love yourself – inside and out – body, mind, and soul. You'll discover how to embrace your queenly individuality. You'll understand how you can let go of seeking approval from others while you build your belief in yourself.

Queen, Embrace Your Individuality!

⁕

*L*iving authentically entails going past accepting yourself and actually loving who you are. A good start to this process is to embrace your uniqueness.

Maybe you feel discomfort about being so different from everyone else. Or perhaps you find yourself similar to others to the point that you believe you're boring.

Either way, it's time to recognize that *your special variety of character traits combine to create a one and only, very unique you.*

Although there are many ways to embrace who you are, check out these strategies to open your arms to the amazing individual you are:

1. **Take note of your habits.** What kind of habits do you practice? Do you floss your teeth every night and consistently wash dishes as soon as you dirty them? Is your bedtime and time for arising always the same?

- Understand what's important to you by noticing the behaviors you routinely do. ***In a sense, your habits are your "trademark."***

2. **Describe your personality in detail.** A wonderful technique for embracing your individuality is to think deeply about the type of person you are. If you had to describe yourself to another human being, what words would you use?

- Maybe you're always in a hurry or like to keep a very clean house. Perhaps you have a lot of friends and are quite gregarious.

- Write down your description of yourself and be as thoughtful and thorough about your personality characteristics as you can. ***You're worth the time this strategy will take.***

3. **What is so great about you?** Of course, you have your own special blend of positive qualities, like being a good listener, having a good sense of humor, and being dependable for others.

4. **Identify your biggest struggles.** What challenges you? If you're ever stumped about how to handle a situation, describe those situations on paper. Getting a handle on what taxes you the most increases your self-awareness.

5. **Work to improve how you handle your biggest struggles.** Yes, identification is great but tackling each challenge one by one to experience success in those areas is very important to do for yourself. Why? Because you'll see that you can overcome anything you set your mind to. Delve into self-improvement to learn more about the unique person you are.

6. **Remind yourself that you're a decent human being.** In order to embrace your individuality, you must accept who you are. *Learning to love yourself and take yourself as you are is a great aid to loving and encouraging others.* Sure, you have flaws, but who doesn't?

- Keep in mind that recognizing you're okay doesn't mean you can't work to improve. In fact, accepting your foibles and less-than-perfect characteristics can help you improve.

7. **Vow to embrace who you are each morning.** It's a new day. You have opportunities to experience discoveries about yourself and who you are. Consider the unfolding day as a venue to keep learning more and more about yourself.

Actively work each day to love your individuality. Notice your habits. Stay in close touch with the elements of your personality. Know what is great about you as well as what kinds of things vex you.

Celebrate Your Quirky Side and Thrive

We all have quirks. Maybe you collect vegetables shaped like movie stars or love to recite Old Norse poetry. *Discover more freedom by learning to accept yourself and the idiosyncrasies that make you special.*

Benefits of Celebrating Your Quirky Side

1. **Live authentically.** You can make your own decisions instead of going along with the crowd. Spend time on activities that are meaningful for you, regardless if they're viewed as quirky. *Let your genuine nature shine through.* You'll attract friends who appreciate your true personality.

2. **Boost your confidence.** Feel comfortable with yourself. Take pleasure in who you are and what you do. Be driven by your passions regardless of whether they match the current trends.

3. **Develop your skills.** Your quirks may be trying to tell you something. Use them to identify your natural talents. Maybe you have a flair for needle work or electronics.

4. **Become more tolerant.** *Coming to terms with your own peculiarities can help you to be more open-minded about those around you.* Show your support for a coworker who is learning to play the harpsichord or training for a hula hoop competition.

5. **Enjoy free entertainment.** Your quirks can provide more amusement than cable TV. Feel free to laugh at yourself. Invite your friends to join you.

6. **Manage stress.** Your odd habits may also offer clues about constructive ways for you to relieve the stresses of daily life. Do you find yourself turning to music or cooking when you feel anxious?

How to Embrace Your Quirky Side

1. **Examine your eccentricities.** *Distinguish between strange habits that are harmless and those that may be creating difficulties for yourself and others.* For example, binge drinking may require professional intervention. On the other hand, repairing clocks is a rewarding hobby.

2. **Accommodate others.** Even if your quirks are innocent in themselves, you may need to limit the exposure for others. Your spouse will thank you for whistling in the shower instead of at the dinner table.

3. **Turn down the volume.** Quiet time and solitude will help you get in touch with your quirky side. Find out what you like to do when no one is watching. Observe how you tackle challenges or organize a complex task.

4. **Look back in time.** Thinking back to your childhood can also be revealing. You may find that you have hidden interests that go beyond your professional or family life. Have you always loved cats or been fascinated by machinery?

5. **Question conventional wisdom.** *Independent thinking triggers all kinds of breakthroughs.* Your innovative approach to a project at work could create a better customer experience or reduce processing time. Your friends may be inspired by the novel way you tie a scarf or how you clean your bathroom.

6. **Broaden your experiences.** Having the courage to be original can lead to adventures. *As you try new things, you'll increase your knowledge about yourself and your surroundings.* Your personality

will grow richer.

7. **Develop informed opinions.** Keep in mind that some opinions are more valuable than others. Elaborate reasons for why you prefer red cabbage over green is probably unnecessary. On the other hand, be prepared with facts if you want to persuade your boss to try your unusual filing system for monthly invoices.

8. **Lighten up.** Most of all, relax and let go of rigid expectations. There are many ways to be an outstanding parent, friend, or neighbor. *Follow your quirks to design the path that best suits your unique abilities.*

Quirks make you more interesting and accomplished. Celebrate them! Independent thinking opens up more opportunities for you. Use your quirks to expand your future.

Embracing your individuality will enrich your life in ways you can't imagine!

The next few lessons in your journey toward living authentically will show you several more techniques to help you embrace the awesome individual you are! You'll learn to trust yourself as you stop seeking the approval of others. You'll believe in yourself instead of comparing yourself to others. And you'll learn to love yourself inside and out!

The next lesson will show you how you can avoid approval-seeking behaviors.

Here's what you need to do today:

Take note of your habits. In your journal, make a list of your habits. Which ones are helpful? Which ones do you think you might want to tone down to accommodate others?

How will you do this?

Get started by going to your online course and completing this lessons Affirmations and Self-Reflections:

- I Am Beautiful Inside And Out
- I Am My Own Unique Self Special Creative And Wonderful

Queens Don't Seek Approval From Their Court

These next two lessons take into account how you behave around others – to your own detriment. It's harder to love yourself when you seek the approval of those around you instead of trusting yourself, or compare yourself to them instead of believing in yourself. Today, we'll look at approval-seeking behaviors.

No one is sure how the need for approval developed. *Some social scientists believe that it evolved from a survival advantage that group acceptance provided.* It was challenging to survive 10,000 years ago, and maybe impossible to survive alone. Those that crave acceptance had a better chance of remaining with the group and survival.

Those that didn't care about upsetting others found themselves kicked to the prehistoric curb and an early demise.

In this day and age, though, approval-seeking behavior is self-sabotaging. Trying to impress others is exhausting and minimizes your own importance and individuality.

Free yourself from the need to receive approval from others:

1. **Give your opinion freely.** One symptom of approval-seeking tendencies is the hesitance to share your opinion. You might say something that the other person doesn't approve of. And since it was your opinion, they might not approve of you either.

- Give your opinion, even if it makes you uncomfortable. Start with smaller things. Do you think it will rain? Do you prefer basketball or football? Which movie would you like to see?

2. **Avoid judging others.** If you're overly critical of others, it's only natural that you assume others are the same towards you. By avoiding this type of behavior in yourself, you'll drop the assumption that everyone else is judging you. Allow others to be as they are. It makes life more interesting. Sit back and enjoy the differences.

- Notice your thoughts. Are you constantly judging others in a variety of situations? *You'll fear the judgments of others if you continue to be judgmental.*

3. **Realize that disapproval can be used as a weapon.** Many people use disapproval as a means of getting what they want. They may disapprove of your opinion, clothing, hairstyle, or anything else to enjoy the fruits of your submission.

- Call people on their disapproval of you. Ask them to explain themselves. *Remember that most negative people are looking*

123

for a victim, not a fight. When you stick up for yourself, many of the bullies disappear.

- Knowing this can free you from seeking the approval of others. In many cases, they're just in the game for themselves.

4. **Be aware of what happens when someone disapproves of you.** *Nothing happens.* We seem to be born with an intense desire to fit in. But what actually happens when someone disapproves of you? The sky doesn't fall on top of you. You might suffer from a little anxiety or embarrassment, but it passes.

5. **Do some things for yourself.** If you're constantly seeking approval, you're not taking very good care of yourself. Show yourself that you're important by focusing some of your time and energy on yourself. It might be a little bit uncomfortable at first. You might even feel selfish.

6. **Fill your life with things that are important.** If you had to run across the street naked to save your child's life, you wouldn't be worried about anyone's opinion. That's because your child's life is more important than your ego. But you don't need a disaster to experience this.

- Volunteer with an organization that's doing important work. Write a book that you believe will change lives for the better. Find ways to spend your time on things you consider to be important.

- You'll find that you enjoy more freedom in the other, less important, parts of your life.

Being overly concerned about the opinions of others is damaging to your self-esteem. ***Each time you seek approval, you're diminishing your own importance.*** You're causing yourself pain. Your opinion matters. Allow your individuality to be seen and experienced by others.

In the next lesson, we'll explore the flaw of comparing yourself to others.

Here's what you need to do today:

Avoid judging others. In your journal, write down one person that you may have judged prematurely. Did you have all the facts when you formed your opinion of them? What other facts could have a bearing on their behavior?

Now think of other people that you know. Do you have a habit of automatically judging others and situations in which you find yourself? If so, then you may be diminishing your own importance by automatically thinking that others are judging you also.

What can you do to practice keeping an open mind instead of automatically judging others?

Today is a choose your own adventure for this lessons affirmation and self-reflection. Login in to Prince, Not Required and you can choose to do one or all five, but the point is to do what will enable you to live by your own approval instead of others.

The Rotten Apple Curse of Comparing Yourself to Others

I n the previous lesson, we looked at approval-seeking behaviors. Today, we explore another self-esteem diminishing behavior: comparing yourself to others.

If you're lacking contentment, it could be because you're comparing yourself to others. You've been on Facebook and seen the pictures of other people living their seemingly exciting lives. *It only takes a moment to find yourself wishing you had someone else's career, body, house, or vacation.* Comparing ourselves to others is a common activity.

But there's a critical flaw in this mental exercise. You simply don't have all the information. Someone might have a great body, but they might be seriously ill. That great vacation might have been paid for with an inheritance after a family member passed away.

A smarter strategy is to compare yourself to your own recent past. How is your figure compared to 6 months ago? How are your finances compared to last year? If you're making progress, congratulate yourself. Most people aren't doing nearly as well. They've weighed the same 210 lbs. and had the same $1,200 in their bank account for the last 20 years.

If your life isn't moving forward, then you ought to take pause and address the situation.

Theodore Roosevelt once said, *"Comparison is the thief of joy."* Think about that statement and decide if it rings true for you.

Check out a few more tips that can free you from unnecessary comparisons:

1. **Catch yourself early in the process.** *As soon as you realize that you're making comparisons to others, shift your focus to something else.*

- You can control your thoughts, so use that ability to your advantage.

2. **Remember that the journey is what matters.** Everyone is on a journey to learn, create, and become something unique. It's an individual experience that isn't impacted by what others are doing or accomplishing.

3. **Comparing yourself to others is a game that can't be won.** There are a lot of people in the world. Through sheer statistics, there will constantly be someone with a more attractive spouse, more money, a better car, or a more interesting life.

- *There's no way to compete with 8 billion people in every facet of life.*

4. **Look to your strengths.** Comparisons tend to focus on our weaknesses. We usually compare our shortcomings against others. Embrace your strengths and be proud. Now use those strengths to your advantage.

5. **List the things you have.** Comparisons highlight the things we lack. It's much more productive to think about the things you do have. Your mood and frame of mind will be better, and you'll be in a better position to compete and succeed.

6. **People only let you see the things that want you to see.** Sure, they'll let you see their new BMW and the vacation pictures from Maui. But you'll never see the tears and fights in the bedroom, or the verbal abuse they take from their mother-in-law. *Keep in mind that social media is primarily used for showing the good, rather than telling the bad.*

7. **It's just a habit.** Our lives are filled with habits, and some of them are harmful. Poor mental habits are restrictive. It's like going through life with the emergency brake on.

- Labeling the tendency to compare as a habit has a powerful advantage because we know that habits can be broken.

Comparing yourself to others is limiting and self-defeating. No one can be expected to compare favorably to the vast number of people in the world. Make an effort to limit your comparisons to your own recent past. Are you making progress or backsliding? If you continue to enhance the important areas, your life is likely to be fulfilling and exciting!

In the next lesson, you'll learn even more strategies for learning to like yourself.

Here's what you need to do today:

Pay particular attention to your thoughts today and tomorrow. Catch yourself quickly when you have a thought that compares you to someone else. Stop that thought in its tracks by replacing it with a short, positive affirmation.

Log in for this lesson's affirmations:

- I Recognize My Talents
- I Refrain From Comparing Myself To Others

8 Queenly Principles

Liking Yourself and Living the Life You Want

*I*n this lesson, we review some important strategies regarding thoughts and behaviors that affect your self-esteem. When you learn to like who you are, you can be confident in presenting the real, authentic you to the world.

When you like the person you are, making life choices becomes easier because you trust your own judgment. You recognize that you have the power to create whatever it is that you want for yourself and your family.

Try these strategies to raise your self-esteem:

1. **Stay in tune with your thoughts.** Notice when you're thinking negatively about yourself. ***When you can identify the types of situations in which you tend to put yourself down, you can then***

do something about them.

2. **Squelch unhelpful thinking.** After you take notice of the situations that trigger those negative thoughts, you can set out to stop such thoughts or at least divert them. Do so by developing your own imagery technique.

- Imagine a stop sign and tell yourself to "stop negativity now."

- Visualize that you're at the beach or your grandmother's house, where you always feel relaxed and self-assured.

- *Another way to quell unwelcome ideas is to seek out something positive in the situations you find challenging.* For example, if you feel you're socially inept, make it a point to help others open up to you by asking questions about their work or hobbies. You'll likely find some common ground for a great conversation.

- Learning to stop negative thinking increases your self-confidence and emphasizes that you choose your own path rather than a recurring, unfocused thought pattern.

3. **Know your strengths.** *Occasionally reflecting on what you're good at will help you see that you're cherished, important, and helpful to yourself and others.* List everything you can think of that you do well. Be generous. If nobody makes a ham sandwich like you do, write it down. If you consistently win at golf, include it.

- Make your list longer and longer. Keep adding to it. Challenge yourself to add one strength a month to your list. As your list grows, so will your positive feelings about yourself.

4. **Underscore your unique or quirky aspects.** If you can recite the name of every major Manga comic book or all the elements on the chemistry table, you're a truly unique individual. Embrace these special talents with the care and attention they deserve. Plus, there's likely someone out there looking for the off-beat talent or knowledge you hold.

5. **Accept your positives and negatives.** Learn to accept the parts of you that you've tried to reject in the past. See those less desirable aspects as insurance that you're a member of the human race.

   • *Personal acceptance helps you see that everything in life has a delicate balance and all parts of you create the very special "you" that you are.*

6. **Stay focused to live your best life**. Although it's wise to be aware of your less than positive aspects, focusing on the good things will help you excel and continue accomplishing your goals. Keep moving ahead.

7. **Every morning, make the decision to be in a "good mood."** It's a lot easier to accept who you are when you feel good about this day. Open yourself to the possibilities around you.

8. **Set goals that you want to accomplish.** Rather than working toward what your parents or friends think you should do, search within yourself what you'd like to work for in life and then go for it. *Life is a lot more fun when you choose what you want.*

Liking yourself allows you to share with others all the good you have in your heart. And the more you do, the more positive energy you have flowing in to your life. Set out today to put these tips into action. You'll enjoy your best life ever!

In the next lesson, you'll learn to believe in yourself.

Here's what you need to do today:

Read the affirmations for this lesson and then in your journal, make a list of your strengths. Keep adding to it. Challenge yourself to add one strength a month to your list. As your list grows, so will your positive feelings about yourself.

Your Queenly Authority

───※◦⟡◦※───

Believe in Yourself

*P*reviously, in the last lesson, we looked at important strategies that help you like yourself. You'll like yourself even more when you can believe in yourself, which we'll explore more fully in this lesson.

Nobody but you can be the final authority on your life. If you don't step up in that role, someone else will try to fill it for you. Empower yourself to stake a claim over your own life.

The phrase, "Believe in yourself," is a common piece of advice. But, what does it really mean? Although part of it is self-confidence, there's a deeper meaning to be found and appreciated.

Believing in yourself is about self-awareness. Deep down, you know what you're able and unable to do. When you believe in yourself, others are unable to pressure you into doing anything you don't want to do. On the other hand, no one can hold you back from doing something you know you can do.

Outside perspective is important, but nobody knows you like you know yourself. With regular introspection, you can build unshakable self-confidence. The Delphic maxim "Know thyself," inscribed for all posterity on the Temple of Apollo, speaks to this truth.

What are your strengths? What are your weaknesses? Only you can answer these questions. *You're the only person in the world who truly knows your capabilities.* Too often, people walk away from opportunities muttering "coulda," "woulda," "shoulda."

The Importance of Self-Esteem

Self-esteem needs to be cultivated, just like a garden. Weeds, in the form of negative self-talk, can creep in at any time. *High self-esteem can help you communicate better, make you more decisive, earn you the respect of others, and allow you to maintain your integrity.*

Increasing your self-esteem becomes an exercise in writing a self-fulfilling prophecy. As you build your confidence, you'll empower yourself to achieve more in your personal and professional lives.

Believe in Yourself

Some think of self-doubt as a monster, greedily sucking away their motivation. This outlook isn't particularly helpful because it sends signals to the subconscious that can strengthen self-doubt even more. Instead, be aware that self-doubt is a part of you that's vulnerable and in need of support.

Take these steps and increase your self-esteem starting now:

1. **Explore self-doubt**. Doubt is part of the human experience, just like joy, fear, and sorrow.

- *If you discover what's at the root of self-doubt and explore that, you may find that the doubt loosens its paralyzing grip.* This will help you stop fighting with yourself, and you can move toward your goals.

- The key is to get to the bottom of your insecurities and face your fears. Addressing your fears is easier if you itemize them first. Putting your fears down on paper puts them in perspective.

2. **Take stock of your fears**. Your fears will appear menacing when they're staring at you from within your own mental space.

- *Record your fears daily, in a journal, and watch the list shrink before your eyes.*

3. **Pay attention to your thoughts.** Another way that you can cultivate self-confidence is to listen to your internal dialog.

- Your fears can lurk in the words you use to describe yourself. Instead of saying, "I won't be good at this," try, "How can I make myself better?" out for size.

- **Consider separating yourself from chronically negative people.** Cutting ties with toxic people is difficult, but do what's best for you. Becoming assertive will allow you to help yourself and others.

4. **Relish your successes, but avoid living in the past.** When you're feeling down, it's easy to focus on your failures. Instead, recall your past successes. It's okay to feel grateful for all that you have.

- Maintaining an optimistic mindset will help you recognize opportunities when they arise.

Ultimately, believing in yourself means claiming self-authority. ***Avoid letting others make decisions for you or limit your potential.*** More often than not, these people are projecting their own self-doubts onto you. Focus on your goals and talents, and remember: you deserve success.

7 Tips to Get Your Mind on Your Side

Self-belief isn't optional. It's vital. Think of all the things you haven't accomplished or tried because you didn't have enough belief in yourself. Self-doubt will always creep in at times. That's why it's so important to have an excess of belief in yourself.

Create a reserve of self-belief and you really can accomplish nearly anything you can imagine. What would you do if you believed you could do essentially anything? How would your life be different? How would you feel?

If you need a little more faith in yourself, try these tips:

1. **Examine your beliefs.** You weren't born with any limiting beliefs. You learned every single one of them. We all learn to limit ourselves unfairly. ***Give yourself the credit you deserve.***

   • Think about the limiting beliefs you already have. Do what you can to discard them. Ask yourself if this limiting belief is really legitimate. Where did it come from? What evidence do you have that it simply isn't true?

2. **Give yourself an unlimited number of opportunities to be successful.** It's easy to be filled with doubt if you think you only have once chance to get it right. Give yourself permission to "fail" as many times as necessary. Learn something from each attempt. This is a great way to build self-belief.

3. **Eliminate self-criticism.** As soon as self-doubt starts to invade your thoughts, ask yourself where that inner critic is coming from.

   • Are you channeling a negative experience from the past?

   • Is the source of this criticism credible? It rarely is.

- It can be challenging to quiet your mind, but that doesn't mean you have to let it drag you down. Focus on positive self-talk.

4. **Trust and love yourself.** *For one month, try being your best friend instead of your worst enemy.* How do you treat your best friend or your children? Probably a lot better than you treat yourself. Give yourself the gift of kindness.

5. **Coach yourself.** Everyone needs a little support and encouragement. So when you find yourself struggling, consider what you would say to someone that you really believed in if they were feeling the same way you are. When self-doubt starts to creep in, take a few minutes to coach yourself.

6. **Think about how you would like to act.** Think about how you would think and behave if you were full of self-confidence.

- You can effectively borrow traits from others, too. Who are some of your heroes? Sometimes it easier to imagine others dealing with a situation than to imagine ourselves. *See yourself acting the way your hero would act.*

7. **Remember all your past victories.** We've all accomplished some pretty impressive things, but we're quick to forget them. Grab a pen and some paper and list all the successes you've experienced in life, no matter how great or small.

- If you need help, ask a trusted friend or family member. You might be surprised at what you hear.

Self-belief isn't about becoming arrogant or turning a blind-eye to one's flaws. ***The belief you have in yourself needs to be focused on what you wish to become.*** You can have weaknesses. Everyone does. But there is value in being relaxed about your weaknesses and working to strengthen them.

A strong belief in yourself is a sure ticket to living authentically. You can make it easier to believe in yourself by learning to love yourself inside and out – mind, body, and soul. Your next few lessons of your journey will guide you toward a wonderful self-love. We'll start with loving your body.

Here's what you need to do today:

Think of a recent situation in which you acted in some way that maybe you just thought you should, or went along with the crowd against your beliefs. Describe this situation in your journal. If you were acting strictly in accordance with your beliefs, how would you have acted differently?

Complete this lessons affirmations and ponder on how can you practice what you would like to do differently in similar situations in the future?

Loving Your Physical Self

Looking After Your Body

These next few lessons help you learn to love yourself – all of you – through and through – starting with your body.

Your physical appearance and condition reveal so much regarding how you feel about yourself. Do you make special efforts to care for your body each day? When was the last time you spent extra time to improve your personal appearance? In regard to your health, do you regularly visit your doctor and take all medication as prescribed?

Hopefully, the answer to all of these questions is a resounding, "Yes!" If you're on a road of personal growth and healing, you probably work to change unhealthy lifestyle patterns each day.

Here are some ways you can show self-love by tending to your physical body:

1. **Take more time with your appearance.** Most of us could easily spend a few additional minutes during our shower, shave, makeup application, or hair styling.

- Ask yourself: do you notice the condition of your skin each day? Or do you spend your brief minutes in the mirror thinking unkind things about your body? Maybe you could use the time you spend in self-critique doing nice things for yourself instead: a touch more make-up or a bit closer shave can go a long way toward feeling good about yourself.

- *If you want to demonstrate to the world that you love yourself, spend more time on the physical you.* Take pride in yourself and in your appearance. You'll be glad of your efforts and others will notice too.

2. **Make a change.** Occasionally, do something different with your appearance.

- Get a haircut and style it into that sassy hairdo picture you saved.
- Change the color of your hair.
- Consider trying out a new style of clothing.
- You can even change your eye makeup. YouTube has lots of video tutorials for different looks.

When you alter something about your appearance, you demonstrate you're worth the time and effort it takes to try something new. Plus, it's refreshing. Even if you decide not to stick with a new look, trying one out for a day or a week can bring new zest to your life.

3. **Put energy into yourself.** Knowing you're worthy of your own energy is an important aspect of loving yourself. When you direct your attention toward something that's just for you, even if only for ten minutes a day, the message you send to yourself is that you're worth it.

- Having a partner and a family can be a huge drain on your energy in an average day. *Conserving at least some of your energy for yourself shows you care about you as much as you do your family.*

4. **Notice your physical "positives."** Take a good, honest look in the mirror. Instead of focusing on what you'd change, draw your attention to what you like. Maybe it's your handsome chiseled chin or how you smile with your eyes.

- Acknowledge to yourself what you're proud of physically. Maybe you've got long legs or a really strong core. Perhaps you like of the curve of your waist or your 6-pack abs.

- Take plenty of time to do your physical inventory to find attributes to love about yourself. To feel even better, think about how you can enhance your best features. As you learn more about and augment your positive physical attributes, you'll discover self-acceptance, and be well on your way toward self-love.

5. Sleep more. Unless you're one of the lucky ones, you're most likely on the short end of getting enough sleep. Strive for seven to eight hours each night to show love to yourself.

- Acknowledge that obtaining proper rest and sleep is on your priority list. And related to item #3, above, the more sleep you get the more energy you'll have. And that means more enthusiasm and love to give to your family and to yourself.

6. Brighten up. Wear a color you've never worn before. Something as simple as stepping up your wardrobe a bit indicates that you love yourself. Whether it's a blazer in that new dark teal shade or a print shirt that looks fresh, break into a new color scheme to show you're worth the effort to experiment with new ideas.

7. Ask yourself what your body requires. Perhaps for the first time in your life, seriously ask yourself what type of nourishment your body really needs. If you don't know, see a nutritionist. It's worth the cost of one or two office visits to find out what your body requires to be as healthy as possible.

- *If you already know what your physical self needs, apply your knowledge.* Feed your body what it requires. Making your body a priority is a wonderful and important way to show love to yourself.

8. Consistently focus on your physical self. As long as your doctor approves, exercise in some form at least five days a week. *Your body will feel better and better over time.* Take some time to familiarize yourself with the flexibility of your limbs, the strength of your body's core, and the shape and efficiency of your muscles.

- Strive to perform well physically in some specific way, whether it's doing calisthenics, yoga, weight-lifting, or jogging. Experiment with dance or try training for a triathlon. You'll be pleasantly surprised at the feelings of pride, confidence, and care you feel for yourself when you consistently focus on your physical body.

9. **Acknowledge what your body does for you.** One aspect of loving yourself is realizing everything your body allows you to do. Your mobility, your ability to use your hands to manipulate objects, and the energy that sustains you through a challenging day are all thanks to your body.

- Your physical self holds up for you under plenty of pressure on any given day. *Cultivate gratitude for how your body does pretty much everything you require.* Love your body.

10. **Show commitment to loving yourself.** Through your be-haviors every single day, be dedicated to fully accepting yourself. The level at which you ensure that you meet all of your physical requirements helps illustrate how you feel about yourself. Commit to your own self-care.

Tending to your body is one of the primary ways of showing how much you love yourself. Fortunately, there are plenty of ways to demonstrate that you love your body, and there's no need to do all of them in any given day, though you'll feel great if you do.

In the next lesson, you'll see how you can love your emotional self.

Here's what you need to do today:

In your journal, make a list of everything positive that you can think of about your body. Reflect on these positive traits. Feel grateful that you have them, because not everyone does!

Loving Your Emotional Self

Understanding and Respecting Your Own Feelings

P reviously, in the last lesson, we looked at ways that you can use to love your body. Today, we talk about your emotions.

Possibly the single most important facet of loving yourself is taking great care of your emotional self. *What you believe is true about yourself illustrates the degree to which you love and accept yourself.*

Try these tips to love yourself more by taking care of your emotional being:

1. **Accept yourself.** Realize that you're as important, special and worthy as every other human being on earth. Connect deeply with this reality.

- Use this as an affirmation: *"I am important, special and worthy."* Try saying the affirmation out loud. Repeat it. Write it down.

147

Then, read it to yourself. Do this twice per day, once in the morning and once in the evening. Watch for subtle shifts in the way you view yourself.

2. **Journal.** Write in a journal about what you really like about yourself.

- *Journaling helps you connect with all of your strengths.* The time you spend writing down your thoughts is an opportunity to cultivate positivity about all of your best qualities. On an emotional level, you can most easily relate to positive feelings about yourself when you recognize your own strengths.

3. **Claim responsibility for your own life.** Often we try to find external reasons for why something happened, such as, "Why does he keep hurting me?" or, "What makes her think I deserve this treatment?" Instead, take responsibility.

- Ask yourself, "Since I'm responsible for myself, what do I need to do right now to remedy this situation for me?"

- Once you claim responsibility for your own life, you'll fully consider the ramifications of your choices to stay in less than ideal situations. Over time, you'll begin to make decisions to disconnect from people, places and things that consistently harm you in some way.

- *Take the time to consider what's best for you in life. This is an enormous expression of the love you have for your own self.*

4. **Avoid negativity toward yourself.** A person who loves herself avoids sending herself negative messages.

- You can practice avoiding negativity and still acknowledge that no one is perfect. Being human doesn't mean that you deserve scorn, shame, or ridicule. Instead of beating yourself up emotionally, direct your energies toward turning any situation into something positive.

5. **Forgive others.** You'll feel less burdened by unwanted negative feelings when you cultivate forgiveness.

- Of course, it's also okay to decide that even though you forgive someone, continuing to be involved with that person isn't healthy for you. When you forgive them first, however, you can move on without the extra emotional baggage of hurt and angry feelings.

6. **Send out positive vibes to others.** *Show other people how loving, caring and kind you are.* Often, we get immersed in our daily grind and don't notice all the opportunities we have to make someone's day. Showing positivity and kindness toward everyone can be intensely refreshing. When you do this, you make it obvious to others that you love yourself.

7. **Say you're sorry if you are.** Notice within yourself when you've made an error or had a misstep. Then, openly acknowledge it. This

shows you're a genuine, caring human being.

- You'll ultimately feel very good about apologizing when it's required. Saying you're sorry is a deeply satisfying experience that will help you to love and respect yourself even more.

8. **Let go of any negative feelings you hold toward others.** *Cleansing yourself of as much negativity as possible sets you up for success in life.* You feel better emotionally and physically, act more openly toward others, and demonstrate love to yourself. Lighten your emotional load by letting go of negativity.

9. **Have self-respect.** Refuse to allow anyone to emotionally harm you. Set guidelines within yourself about tolerating unsavory treatment from others. Having limits and boundaries is healthy and shows that you protect and respect yourself in all situations.

10. **If you dislike the way someone treats you, leave their presence, if possible.** Doing so will be the gateway toward re-claiming your self-respect and self-love.

- Exit negative relationships, regardless of how scary that may feel. Ultimately, your love for yourself will be stronger than for someone who's less than positive toward you.

In essence, understanding and acknowledging your own feelings validates your existence. By being honest with yourself about your feelings and taking action in accordance with them, you honor and show love to yourself.

In the next lesson, you'll discover how you can love your intellectual self.

Here's what you need to do today:

Forgive someone. Are you having trouble forgiving someone that has hurt you? Take a leap of faith and forgive them. See how this small, but difficult, act lightens your own load and helps to set you free from the negative emotions you've been carrying from this situation.

Loving Your Intellectual Self

❧

Feeding Your Mind

*I*n the two previous lessons, we explored loving your body and emotions. Loving yourself also involves providing your brain with plenty of intellectual stimulation. Here are some effective ways to demonstrate self-love by giving your mind a workout.

1. **Do something you've longed to do.** Loved art class in high school? Always wanted to pick up that paint brush again? Now's the time to go for it. Exploring a new or long-loved subject might feel like a delicious indulgence. ***You deserve to feast your mind on subjects that are intellectually stimulating to you.***

- The internet offers an abundance of fascinating information. Dive into a search on a topic that arouses your interests.

2. **Write down your life priorities.** What's important to you? Next,

jot down your life goals. What do you really seek to accomplish in life? Finally, take note of how you spend most of your time. Your three lists should all be similar or closely connected.

- For example, if you've always wanted to go to college, did you? Do you now spend most of your time achieving that thing you've desired for so long?

- If you want more training to excel at work, do you make sure you follow through to attain it?

- If travel is a dream of yours, do you do something every single day related to it? You'll be intellectually stimulated if you make efforts to achieve your greatest desires.

- ***When you spend your time and thoughts on working toward your goals, your mind will be at its happiest and most fit.*** Plus, this sort of work shows that you care enough about yourself to have your priorities in good order.

3. **Foster your passions and dreams.** Ask yourself, "What do I care intensely about?" Then, delve into that subject. Learn everything you can about it. Practice it. Study it. Live it. If an idea, topic, or endeavor excites you, chase after it. The same goes for your dreams. Once you know what your hearts' desires are, do everything you can to achieve them.

- ***Stay engaged on a daily basis with your life's passions and dreams.*** There's no better way to express self-love than to strive to give yourself what you truly want in life.

4. **Ensure you've got a real life with real people.** When you love yourself, you'll have close friends and family with whom you regularly spend time. Spend this time with your loved ones "in person" rather than with their Facebook pages.

- Connecting with people in the physical world gives you many kinds of opportunities to keep your mind sharp. You'll engage in interesting discussions, be exposed to what's going on in the world, and have a forum to formulate and share your own opinions and intellectual ideas.

5. **Avoid doing things just because "it's always been this way."** Know and connect with your own consciousness. Perform behaviors deliberately and with great forethought. Living consciously shows that you use your mind to think through what you do because you care about what's going on in your life.

- When you live intentionally, you intellectually consider the ramifications of the choices you make. You recognize how precious time is and judiciously spend the twenty-four hours you get in a day on what's most important to you. Now that's real self-love.

6. **Take a personal inventory of your life.** Make a list of your personal characteristics. Then take a piece of paper. Draw a line down the middle. On the left side, write down what's working. On the right side, write down what's not working. Then, make some

decisions about the things you want to change. And then work on them.

- This exercise will help you determine what your "thinking self" requires. Figuring out what you need to be intellectually challenged and move forward in life demonstrates that you're worth the time and effort to be happy.

7. **Consider the bigger picture.** As Mahatma Gandhi once said, "Be the change you want to see in the world." *Use your mind to ponder how you want your life and the lives of others to be.* Strive to behave the way that you hope others will behave. Consciously decide to make the changes that you hope other people will make. Set an excellent example to the world.

- You may wonder how this can be considered self-love, since these actions may seem so intent on affecting other people. But how can you not feel good about yourself when you're focused on making the planet a better place?

8. **Tell yourself you're worthy.** *Recognize that you deserve to be loved, not only by yourself, but by those around you.* Mentally prepare yourself for the love you receive from others and yourself. Know that you're worth of all the love you give to yourself. With the proper mindset, your possibilities in life are limitless.

- Working with your belief in yourself will help pave the way to more self-acceptance and self-love in other areas. You'll find loving yourself to be much easier when you're confident that you're worth the effort.

9. **Find your power.** When you see that you have control over your own mind, you'll be provided with opportunities to do as you wish with your life. In other words, you'll get to exercise the power you have in ways that enrich your existence.

- Closely related to finding your power is infusing knowledge into your daily life. ***When you gain knowledge, you gain power.*** Accessing the power you have in your mind means you'll experience self-confidence and feel love for yourself each day.

Loving yourself means you seek, find and experience all types of mental stimulation. You look into topics of interest, maintain real friendships with real people, live consciously each day, consider the bigger picture, and find power within you. Express your self-love by feeding your mind with intriguing thoughts, ideas and activities.

In the next lesson, you'll learn techniques to help you love your spiritual self.

Here's what you need to do today:

Consider the things you do just because *"it's always been this way."* Connect with your consciousness. Is there something you would like to do differently? Try doing it your way.

Loving Your Spiritual Self

Caring for Your Soul

I n this last lesson in this module about loving yourself, you'll learn the importance of loving your spirit.

Filling your spirit with genuine joy is a must if you love yourself. Give yourself time to do only what you love to do. Try refreshing your living space even in small ways from time to time, disengaging from technology periodically, and doing other activities that bring adventure and joy into your life.

Check out these strategies and be inspired to think of still more ways to demonstrate how you care about yourself:

1. **Make it a good morning.** Take a little time in the morning to do something you really like to do. It might be 45 minutes of yoga to start your day off right. Maybe you'd like to read your favorite novel for 15 minutes before the kids get up. Or perhaps 10 minutes to practice meditation would give you the restful start you need to

have a good day.

- ***Give yourself the gift of the first few minutes of each morning.*** Your whole day will be better and your soul will thank you for that little bit of "me time" when you first arise.

2. **Indulge.** Do a little something special for yourself each and every day. You'll enjoy life more when you put in the effort to do just that one thing that makes your heart sing. Go ahead and do those activities you think are special, fun or self-indulgent.

- You can afford 30 minutes to 1 hour every day just for yourself, can't you? Knowing you deserve it translates into loving yourself.

3. **Change your personal space.** *Making small but meaningful changes in your home truly invigorates your soul.* Nothing says "I love myself" like renewing your cherished space in your house.

- Clean something deeply and well.
- Throw some things away that weigh you down.
- Rearrange the furniture in your living room. If you don't spend much time in your living room, try this in your favorite room, the one in which you hang out the most.
- Paint.

4. **Turn on the tunes.** Listen to your music each day for at least 15 minutes. Most phones today have MP3 players or iPods in them.

5. **Turn off the gadgets.** One day every other week, or even once a month, turn off your cell phone, television and computer.

- *Disconnecting from your technology is a great way to re-connect with your soul.*

- Consider how you might spend a whole day away from all your gadgets. Will you take a walk, bake bread from scratch, or have a relaxing afternoon out in your yard? Maybe you'll spend the day with your father or your niece. Whatever you do with your unplugged time, you'll feel relaxed and rejuvenated.

6. **Allow yourself to feel love from others.** *Experiencing the loving messages given to you by your family members and cherished friends is good for the soul.* For example, when you go out to lunch with your sisters, savor their presence. Take in how they smile and make eye contact with you, or revel in that special silent communication you have.

- Soak up the love that your cherished friends and family provide by staying emotionally in touch with their compliments or by their presence. Although we are often taught not to accept compliments or take them to heart, they're good for you, and are given with love. Accepting them is a way of loving yourself.

7. **Worship.** If you enjoy attending a church, temple, or other place of worship, doing so regularly is good for your soul. If you prefer to pray at home alone, that method of worship will also bring you

soulful comfort and demonstrate self-love.

- Perhaps you seek to discover the "right" place of worship for you. That's okay, too. Finding your spiritual "home" can be a great adventure in self-love. People who want to worship and are successful in finding the place that fits for them re-fill their souls every time they attend the services or events that are meaningful to them.

- ***If you have religion or spirituality that's meaningful in your life, practice it.*** Many people report that worshiping simply makes them feel better.

- If you don't have a spiritual "home," and feel like something's missing in your life, visit various kinds of churches or temples to see if you can fill the void and discover what your soul seeks. Whether you go alone or with friends, you'll have fascinating experiences. And even if you don't find a place for you, you'll learn a lot about yourself.

8. **Immerse yourself in nature.** Make special efforts to experience the joys and beauties of nature. If you've ever walked through a pine tree forest, you know the awesome spiritual power inherent in the great outdoors.

- Whether you put on your snowshoes and tromp off through piles of lovely white fluff or walk along a sandy beach somewhere collecting seashells, find a way to stay involved with nature.

9. **Be adventurous.** Find that part of you that seeks the unknown and strives for the yet-experienced adventure. Maybe you want to climb a mountain, run a sprint triathlon, or visit the pyramids in Egypt. Whatever your adventuresome spirit seeks, make an effort to provide it in some way. You'll feel deeply alive and loved when you do.

10. **Recognize that time is of the essence.** Spend your hours and minutes in ways that demonstrate your self-love. Consider time as precious, golden moments meant to be spent doing the things you love and working toward your life's goals. *Decide to love yourself every single minute of every single day by making each of those moments count.*

Taking care of your spiritual self can be done by practicing one or many of these strategies. Anything that brings joy to your soul ultimately demonstrates self-love.

> **"Your soul is all that you possess. Take it in hand and make something of it!"** – *Martin H. Fischer*

Now that you know, accept, and love yourself, the next part of your journey to authenticity will let you put it all together and start planning an exciting future by discovering your life purpose.

But first, we'll take a pause for summary and reflection of this module about loving yourself.

Here's what you need to do today:

Field trip! Immerse yourself in nature. Take a walk in a nearby park, nature preserve, the mountains, a forest, or a beach. Be mindful of the nature around you. How does it make you feel? How can you include more time in nature as part of your regular schedule?

The Reflection In Your Crown

*I*n your journey to authenticity, you've already discovered your unique traits, talents, skills, values, and passions. You've identified areas that you may want to alter in order to make your life more satisfying. You've accepted your flaws and forgiven yourself for your mistakes. Now, you're ready to embrace your individuality and love who you are!

It's important to let go of behaviors that find you trying to seek the approval of others or comparing yourself to them. As a unique individual, you are every bit as "good" as any of them. Realize how much in you there is to like and recognize your own value in this world!

Develop a strong belief in yourself. Learn to trust your own judgment. Begin to make choices based on your own likes, dislikes, and values. Start planning your goals and future according to what you desire – not what someone else wants for you.

Finally, discover how to love all of you – inside and out! Learn how to love your body, emotions, intellect, and spirit. See how you can take action each day to take care of yourself and show yourself and the world that *you* are important.

Self-Reflection Questions:

How does loving myself help me live authentically?

What types of situations cause me to hide who I really am? What can I do to embrace the truly unique parts of me?

How can I practice learning to trust my own judgment?

Self-Reflection Exercises:

Complete the exercises in the workbook called "Loving Yourself Workbook." This workbook will help you learn how to love yourself, inside and out.

Now that you know, accept, and love yourself, get ready for some fulfilling strategies in the next module as you learn your life purpose.

Wearing Your Self-Love Crown Proudly Quiz

❦

1. Does toning down your quirky side to accommodate others mean that you don't love yourself?

- a. Yes
- b. No

2. What usually happens when someone disapproves of you?

- a. You have to take out the trash
- b. You miss your favorite TV show
- c. The world thinks less of you
- d. Nothing

3. Which strategy is smarter than comparing yourself to others?

- a. Comparing yourself to your own recent past

- b. Avoiding other people
- c. Making a high salary so you'll always feel like you're better than others
- d. All of the above

4. Which strategy can help you stop negative thoughts?

- a. Imagining a stop sign
- b. Visualizing your "happy" place, like the beach or your grandma's house
- c. Looking for the silver lining
- d. All of the above

5. Who truly knows your capabilities?

- a. Your boss
- b. Your spouse
- c. You
- d. All of the above

6. Which idea is true about limiting beliefs?

- a. We were born with limiting beliefs.
- b. We learned our limiting beliefs.
- c. You can't overcome a limiting belief. You just have to work around it.
- d. A limiting belief doesn't affect your potential.

7. Imagining how you would like to act in certain situations can increase your belief in yourself.

- a. True
- b. False

8. Which activity can increase your love for yourself?

- a. Taking care of your appearance
- b. Writing in your journal
- c. Scheduling more time to do things you like to do
- d. All of the above

9. When you believe that you deserve to be loved, what is a likely outcome?

- a. You'll fall in love
- b. Others will be more likely to love you
- c. Both A & B
- d. Neither. What you believe about yourself doesn't have anything to do with anyone else.

10. Spending time in nature, like the beach, mountains, or a forest, can increase your love for yourself.

- a. True
- b. False

V

The Self-Love Workbook

Every day, you have a multitude of opportunities to love yourself. **Whether it's taking care of yourself physically in some way, finding intellectual stimulation, carefully managing your emotions, or feeding your soul, show you love yourself in everything you do.** *This workbook will aid you in discovering new ways to show yourself some love.*

Your Physical Self

Looking After Your Own Body

How do you feel about your appearance?

Strategy: Accepting yourself just the way you are will actually help you in pursuing your goals.

* * *

What are your strongest physical points and features?

Strategy: Make a conscious decision to love yourself, no matter what.

* * *

Think about ways you can change something about your physical appearance/condition. Write them here.

Strategy: Rome wasn't built in a day. Set small goals to experience success in your quest to improve your physical appearance and condition.

* * *

Are there certain activities you love to do but just don't have the time or energy to do them on a daily basis? If so, what are those activities?

Strategy: Tell yourself you're worth the time and effort to do what you want to do for yourself.

* * *

Commit to yourself now to make time for a couple of those activities each day. Write here when and how you will fit them into your day.

Strategy: Make time each day for a beloved activity. Even though you might not see the value in having a hobby, you'll feel special and enjoy your day more when you do an activity you love to do.

* * *

From this day forward, how will you focus on your physical self in these 2 areas: nutrition and exercise. Be specific in what you will do.

Strategy: Place a sticky note on your bathroom mirror with your brief plan to "eat more fruit" or "walk 30 minutes." Also, place a duplicate note on your refrigerator as an extra reminder.

Your Intellectual Self

Properly Feeding Your Mind

What are your priorities in life?

Strategy: Ponder what you truly want your life to be like. Then develop a strategy to make it happen.

List your life goals here. Focus on your top 5 goals.

Strategy: Be specific when writing your goals. Instead of, "Get a job promotion," write, "Complete the 4 week accounting training and get a pay increase within 6 months from today."

* * *

Are you satisfied with the number of friends (real life friends, not online) you have? When was the last time you got together with friends? Set a goal now about how you'll spend more time with loved ones over the coming months.

Strategy: Call a friend or family member to make a plan to spend time together at least every other week.

* * *

Do a personal inventory. List what you love about your life here.

Now, list what you'd like to change about your life. Focus on how to make your intellectual life better.

Strategy: Consider whether getting new training or learning something new would be a welcome change to your life.

***

Do you feel you deserve love? Why or why not?

Strategy: Recognize that you matter. Because you're here on earth, you deserve to love and be loved.

Your Emotional Self

Understanding and Respecting Your Own Feelings

What does it mean to you to take responsibility for your own life?

Strategy: Think about times when you simply stayed in

a relationship because it was easier. Now, consider what it would have been like if you had taken full responsibility for how your life progressed.

* * *

When you "talk" to yourself, what do you say? Is it mostly positive and encouraging? If not, why not?

Strategy: Make it a point to arrest any negative thinking and replace it with a positive thought. Instead of, "I messed up," think, "I'll do better next time."

* * *

Do you apologize when you're aware you made an error? If not, why not? Do you forgive others? If you don't, think about why not and write those reasons here.

Strategy: Saying you're sorry shows you accept the fact that you sometimes make mistakes. It's an important step to self-love. Also, letting go of hurt and forgiving others will free you emotionally.

* * *

Do you respect yourself?

If someone mistreats you, what do you do? How do you handle it?

Strategy: One who loves herself has self-respect. She has limits in terms of how she allows someone to treat her. Sometimes, loving yourself means you respect yourself enough to change a disappointing or hurtful situation.

Spiritual Self

Caring for Your Soul

Have you been thinking about changing your personal **space somehow?** How would you do it? What changes would you make?

Strategy: Renew your soul by transforming a special space in your home.

* * *

How much off-work time in an average day do you spend with technology?

If you aren't sure, pledge to keep track tomorrow of your time spent with gadgets.

Strategy: Explore new hobbies or revive an old one with your new-found time.

Are you open to feeling loved from friends and family members?

Strategy: Be aware and accepting of the love that people give you.

* * *

How often do you go outdoors just to enjoy the day?

Name some simple ways you can enjoy nature every day or two.

Strategy: Find the beauty in nature each day. You'll find your spirits are lifted and you approach your day more positively. And you'll love yourself even more.

* * *

Do you have adventure in your life? If not, why not? How can you add some adventure to your existence?

Strategy: Having an adventure from time to time will boost your soul. Try it.

"Your heart knows your song, but you have to be will-ing to listen to the words." ~Sue Rock

VI

Determining Your Role as Monarch

Now that you've fully accepted your crown, know love, and embrace who you are, you're ready to begin planning a future kingdom that will truly make you happy. This module will give you strategies that will lead you to discover your life purpose and incorporate it into your plans, goals, and daily life.

The Fairytale of Discovering and Living Your Life Purpose

*P*reviously in your journey to queenly authenticity, you've discovered who you really are and learned to love yourself through and through. This module focuses on strategies to reveal your life purpose to you so you can arrange your life around what is most important to you.

Do you wake up each day dreading the idea of spending another day at work? You might even feel the need to be a part of something bigger and more meaningful. ***If you've failed to discover and build your life around your life purpose, you might feel dissatisfied with your life.*** Determining the purpose of your life can be a simple process.

It can take a bit of work to uncover the truth, but it's within you. It's waiting to be unearthed and utilized.

Living a life that's congruent with your purpose will allow you to start each day with a smile, hope, and a plan. It's a tool for connecting with something meaningful outside yourself. Everyone has a different "why". The trick is to determine the "why" that fits your values and talents.

If your life is in a rut, discovering your life purpose is the first step to a life filled with passion and contentment.

"The purpose of life is to live it, to taste experience to the utmost, to reach out eagerly and without fear for newer and richer experience."

Eleanor Roosevelt

Maybe you hold the belief that work is called "work" for a reason. You might think that life is hard, boring, and that enjoyment is only for children and retirees. *All stages of life can be meaningful and exciting.* Knowing that you're living the life that's right for you is the key to finding enjoyment each day.

The advantages of knowing your life purpose are far reaching:

1. **You'll enjoy focus and clarity.** When you're not spending your time and efforts on the things that matter to you, your focus is elsewhere. When you're not clear on your purpose, it's hard to make effective decisions.

   • Lacking direction, focus, and purpose is no way to go through life. Knowing your purpose makes life simpler.

2. **Life will be more fun!** When you know your purpose and live it each day, life has the opportunity to be more enjoyable. With your fears and doubts in the rearview mirror, you're in a better position

to enjoy yourself.

3. **It enhances your passion for life.** *Spending your day on the things that are most important to you will release your passion.* You'll feel the enthusiasm you had as a child. With a compelling future and a high level of motivation, you become unstoppable. This is missing from a life without a clear purpose.

4. **You become part of something bigger than yourself.** You'll have sense of certainty that's both comforting and peaceful. It's a chance to make a big and meaningful contribution to the world.

Discovering the answer to the question, *"What is the purpose of my life?"* will change your life forever. How can you determine your life purpose?

As you'll see, there are several strategies.

In the next lesson, you'll explore the answers to some very important questions that may reveal your life purpose to you.

Here's what you need to do today:

Reflect on how your life may change by discovering your life purpose. Start with 'A Guide to Discovering Your Purpose.' It's available in your Prince, Not Required course.

In your journal, write three ways in which your life will be different and more satisfying to you.

Mini-Quests to Reveal the Purpose of Your Life

~∽✦∽~

*T*o recap, the last lesson had you discovering the benefits of finding out your life purpose. This module will give you many strategies to find your life purpose. Today, we'll go over some important questions that can reveal your purpose to you.

It's impossible to find your purpose without a degree of self-reflection. **Answers are the result of asking questions.** Asking the right questions will provide the answers you seek. When you ask yourself questions, it's imperative to listen to the answers. The response you receive can be very subtle and quiet. Keep an open mind.

Be sure to record your answers!

Ask yourself these useful questions:

1. **If you only had a year to live, how would you spend it?** With the clock ticking, we're much more able to focus on the important stuff and let everything else go.

- The things that come to mind are worthy of further consideration. Could you spend your life engaged in one of these ideas?

- Just reminding yourself that you're going to die one day can be helpful. The reminder that your time is limited can reduce the habit of wasting time and being indecisive.

2. **How do you want others to remember you?** What would you like your obituary to say? How would you like your children, friends, and other family members to remember you?

- Make a conscious decision about how you'd like others to remember you and put together a plan to live that life.

3. **What did you love to do as a child that you no longer do?** As children, we're quite clear about what we like and don't like. In addition, younger children aren't concerned with the perceptions of others. We do things solely because we like them when we're 6-years old. What have you given up over the years?

- As we become teenagers, social pressure and the need to impress others can steer us away from the things we love.

- In young adulthood, we become overly concerned with the practicality of our choices. *"Can I make enough money at this to have a decent lifestyle?"*

- ***With a little thought, you can find a way to make a living doing what you love.*** Life is short. Consider what you once loved to do and find a way to incorporate it back into your life.

4. **What type of discomfort can I handle?** Everything is awful part of the time. Living your life's purpose will have its disadvantages. What can you handle?

- If you dream of being an artist, musician, writer, or actor, you'll be rejected at least 95% of the time.

- If you want to create a law firm, you'll spend at least a decade working 80-hours each week.

- Do you want to be a teacher? Can you handle the parents and the children that constantly disrupt class?

- *If you can't handle the worst aspects of pursuing your purpose, consider reconsidering your choice.*

5. **What topics and activities make you lose track of time?** Have you ever gotten so involved with a conversation or an activity that you missed a meal or were amazed by how much time had passed?

- Maybe you lose track of time when you play the guitar. However, take another step in your thinking. Is it the guitar specifically or music in general? Is it the guitar or the process of competing with yourself and seeing improvement?

- Make a list of the times you've been so focused that you forgot about everything else.

- Imagine if you had a career that incorporated this phenomenon. You'd never have to "work" another day again!

6. **What do you dream about doing but are too afraid?** Admit it. *There's something you fantasize about, but you can't quite get yourself to take action.* It might be climbing Mount Everest, writing a screenplay, or becoming a doctor.

- Why haven't you taken the first step? In many cases, you'll find your resistance to trying something new is fear. Often, it's the fear of failing, especially failing in front of others.

- Keep in mind that the only way to become good at something is to work through the initial period of being bad at it. It's unlikely that your first script will be purchased. In fact, it will probably be awful. But the next attempt will be better. It takes time to become good at a new skill.

- *The more embarrassment you can handle, the greater your ultimate success.*

7. **How could you best serve the world?** Of all the challenges that exist in the world, how could you best solve one of them?

- True happiness requires contributing to something outside yourself.

- It's not possible to solve any of the world's problems alone. You'll be forced to work constructively and creatively with others. This could be the kind of fulfillment you seek.

- Make of list of all the ways your skills, interests, and talents could benefit the world in a meaningful way.

Did you ask yourself every question? Did you record your answers?

How can you use the answers to enhance your life?

Introspection is a necessary part of finding your life purpose. Ask yourself the important questions and listen to the answers.

In the next lesson, you'll discover how you may find the purpose you seek in your journal!

Here's what you need to do today:

You'll get the most from this lesson by answering all of the questions presented above. Put the questions and answers in your journal. To dive even deeper, complete '*7 Ways To Discover Your Life Purpose*' in your online course.

Find Your Queenly Purpose Through Writing

n your quest to discover your life purpose, you previously answered some important questions about your purpose. This lesson is an exercise in brainstorming for your purpose.

Most of us don't enjoy writing. We'd much rather think things through, but writing can be a very powerful tool. *Your perspective can change when you see your ideas on paper.* Allowing a little light to shine on your thoughts and ideas can provide clarity. Dust off your notebook and take pen to paper.

Writing is a powerful tool that can permit a dialog with your subconscious:

1. **You'll need a clean sheet of paper, a pen, and a quiet place for sixty minutes.** You might not need a full hour.

- A word processor is an acceptable substitution to a pen. However, writing by hand is preferable.

2. **Empty your mind of your preconceived ideas.** Part of the reason you've been unable to discover the purpose of your life is your erroneous thinking. We limit ourselves far too much. The answers often lie in places we never bother to look. Keep an open mind.

3. **Write, *"What is my life purpose?"* at the top of the page.** This sets the stage and informs your subconscious of your purpose.

4. **Write whatever comes to mind.** You might think, *"This is a dumb idea."* That's fine. Write it down. Avoid judging any of your thoughts.

5. **Expect that it will take 15 minutes to rid yourself of your mental clutter.**

6. **Stick with the process.** At some point, you'll want to quit or do something else instead. There's no reason to be fearful of learning the truth. Fight through the discomfort.

7. **Continue writing until you find it.** How will you know? You'll know. You'll probably even cry. Just keep writing until you're certain you've found it.

   • Go with the answer that provides the greatest emotional surge.

Ensure that others won't interrupt you during the process. Any significant interruption would require starting the process over from the beginning. ***Most people that attempt this exercise will quit before reaching the end.*** Be one of the few that completes the process.

Give it a chance. You have nothing to lose.

Brainstorming can be a powerful method to find your purpose. If you're still searching, the next lesson will explain how you can meditate on your life purpose.

Here's what you need to do today:

Your journal is an excellent place to collect your thoughts on your life purpose. Start a new page in your journal and at the top of the page, write: *"What is my life purpose?"* Brainstorm this topic and write down everything that comes to mind.

Meditate to Unlock the Queen Inside

❦

*I*n previous lessons, you considered your answers to some important questions and did some brainstorming in the search for your life purpose. This lesson will show you how you can use meditation to reveal your purpose to you.

Meditation isn't just for the Yogis and Buddhist monks of the world. Meditation has been around for thousands of years. ***Meditation and mindfulness have never been more popular than they are today.*** It's now a tool used by medical professionals in a variety of fields and in the business world. Prisons are even teaching meditation to inmates.

Meditation is an acquired skill that requires time and effort to master. There's no better time to get started than today.

Use meditation to reveal your life purpose:

1. **Sit comfortably in a quiet place free of distractions.** The ideal sitting position is one you can hold without repositioning. A firm, comfortable chair is the best option for most people. If you're

physically able to sit in a lotus position, that's even better.

2. **Maintain a focus on your breath.** Feel the air moving in your nose and out of your mouth. Continue doing this for at least 10 minutes.

- Maintaining a focus on your breath is much more challenging than you think! Your mind will wander constantly. There's no cure other than practice.

3. **Ask yourself, "Why am I here? What is my purpose in life?"** Then relax and listen to the answers your higher self provides.

- *As with the writing exercise, you might get many nonsensical answers at first. Keep with it.*

4. **Repeat this process each day.** It might take a few days to discover the answer. Meditate on a regular schedule and continue to ask yourself the appropriate questions. Continue the process until you receive an answer that makes intuitive sense to you. It will simply feel "right".

5. **Take advantage of guided meditation.** There are many videos on YouTube of guided meditations with the goal of finding your life purpose. Of course, there are other products available, too.

- Guided meditation can be much easier for the beginning meditator. Consider trying this process.

There are countless books, videos, and audio programs dedicated to meditation. ***Experiment and find the most effective method for you.*** Guided meditation can be an excellent process for anyone that wishes to begin meditating.

Still stumped on your life purpose? If so, the next lesson will prompt your introspection with some further questions.

Here's what you need to do today:

Today, try meditating on your life purpose. Follow the steps as shown in the lesson. For further direction login to Prince, Not Required and learn the *'6 Benefits of Introspection'* and how *'Quiet Moments Allow You To Connect With Your Soul.'*

7 More Quests to Reveal Your Life Purpose

*I*n previous lessons, we went over some questions that may help you find your life purpose and tried out some strategies that may help, including journaling and meditating.

If the previous approaches haven't satisfied your quest, there are additional questions you can answer. ***While meditation and writing can be highly effective, some of us have greater success with more conventional means.*** Avoid giving up. There's too much at stake to stop.

Spend a few minutes on each question before moving on to the next:

1. **What are your greatest regrets?** Which missed opportunities do you regret the most? Is there a skill you wish you had started learning years ago? What decisions would you change if given a second chance?

• What career would choose if you could go back in time and be 18-years old again? Is it really too late now?

2. **Who inspires you the most?** Think about the people that fill you with feelings of respect and admiration.

- What is it about them that inspires you? Could you incorporate some of these same qualities in yourself? Could you live a similar life?

3. **What are your natural talents?** In what areas have you always excelled? Do you understand complex ideas? Is it your social skills? Are you musically talented? Are you compassionate and considerate?

- *While you can learn to be good at anything, you can save a lot of time if you're able to put your natural abilities to work.* Imagine the progress you'd make after 10 years of effort using your natural abilities rather than starting from scratch.

- If you believe that you were born with a particular purpose, it only makes sense that the necessary talents would be provided to you, too.

4. **What makes you feel good about yourself?** If you could spend most of your time doing things that make you feel great, your life would be pretty wonderful!

- Create a list of all the things you do that make you feel good about yourself.

5. **If you had to teach a subject, what would you choose?** It's only enjoyable to teach subjects that you like. The subject you'd like to teach is a good candidate for your life purpose.

6. **In what areas do people ask you for help?** Most of us wouldn't ask a homeless person for stock tips. We ask people for advice that we believe have a level of expertise higher than our own.

- Do others constantly ask you for relationship advice?

- Do people ask you about spiritual matters?

7. **Imagine you're 80-years old, what memories do you want to have?** Imagine you're sitting on your front porch swing. What would you like to claim as your past? What type of relationships would you like to have experienced? What do you want to have accomplished?

- *How can you make this ideal past become your present?*

You now have a good idea of your life purpose. The next step, which you'll find in the next lesson, is determining how to incorporate the knowledge into your life.

Here's what you need to do today:

Answer the questions from this lesson in your journal. To get started, the first question is, *"What are your greatest regrets?"*

After that login to Prince, Not Required and complete *'New Ideas for Discovering Your Life's Purpose'*.

Make Your Purpose a Part of Your Kingdom

*t's great that, in the previous lessons, you've narrowed down your primary reason for living, but how can you use that knowledge?

Knowing something has minimal value if you're not applying the knowledge. Focus on making small changes to your daily habits to incorporate your life purpose into your life. Slow progress is the most reliable way to create major change in your life.

Let's suppose your purpose is to help illiterate adults to read:

1. **Look to the future.** What does the end of your journey look like? Are you sitting at the library, helping someone learn to read? Are you in charge of a charity that serves those unable to read? Are you asking Bill Gates for $10,000,000 to fight for your cause?

2. **What can you do today to get started?** Starting is always the hardest part. What can you do today?

- Learn more about illiteracy. What are the statistics? What are the causes? What is the best way to teach an adult to read?

- What local resources are available? Can you contact them for advice?
- Could you put an ad in Craig's List and get started helping someone today?

3. **Remind yourself of your purpose each day.** *Each morning and evening, take a minute to remind yourself of your purpose.* Look to the future and feel excited. This is especially important on those challenging days that inevitably happen from time to time.

4. **Track your progress.** Keep a journal and list your successes and failures. How can you experience more successes and prevent future failures? Appreciate how far you've come.

5. **Spread the word.** If you've found your purpose in life, it's your obligation to let the world know about it. How can you communicate the importance of adult illiteracy to the world? You're not just a worker on this project. You're also a messenger.

Realize that making a big difference requires big effort and time. Avoid letting the magnitude of your dreams overwhelm you. *A little work and attention each day are cumulative.* Your progress will shock you.

Making your life purpose a part of your life is part of living authentically. In the next module, you'll discover many other ways to live an authentic life and even plan a future that you'll love!

But first, we'll pause for summary and reflection of this module.

Here's what you need to do today:

Remind yourself of your purpose each day. On a small card or sticky note, write down your idea of your life purpose. Post this where you'll see it several times each day, such as on your bathroom mirror or your desk.

If you use your computer often, make a digital sticky note to show up on your desktop with your life purpose.

If you leave for work each day, make a couple of copies of your life purpose and post one at home and one at work.

Reflections on Ruling

inding your life purpose changes the direction and emphasis of your life. It also enables you to be an amazing ruler. *If you haven't taken the time to determine the purpose of your life, the quality of your experience on Earth has been limited.* There are many advantages to discovering your unique purpose.

Introspection is a part of making this discovery. Self-reflective questions, meditation, and writing are all potential options. Use every method at your disposal until you're satisfied with the answer you receive.

Would you like to incorporate your life purpose into your career? Today, more than ever, it's possible to make a living doing a wide variety of things. For example, you can live in Alaska and give tuba lessons to a student in Miami via Skype. You can publish your own book without the need for a traditional publisher. Your can make your life purpose a major part of your life.

Find your purpose and reclaim your life!

Self-Reflection Questions:

1. Have I been living my life purpose? Why not?

2. What advantages would I enjoy if I knew the purpose of my life?

3. If I'm hesitant to find my life purpose, why is that?

4. Have I located at least three guided meditations on finding my life purpose?

5. What is my end goal? How will things look when I live my purpose continuously for years?

6. What can I do each day to move toward realizing my vision?

7. How can I monetize my life purpose? Is it necessary?

8. How can finding my life purpose help me live authentically?

Next, you'll be starting the last part of this course, which is about living authentically. The first lesson will give you some important tips on living like a true queen.

Determining Your Role as Monarch Quiz

1. What is an advantage of knowing your life purpose?

   - a. You'll enjoy focus and clarity.
   - b. Life will be more fun.
   - c. It enhances your passion for life.
   - d. All of the above

2. What is the key to finding the most enjoyment each day?

   - a. Knowing that you're living the life that's right for you
   - b. Having a high-paying job
   - c. Living in the biggest house on the street
   - d. Being the boss at work

3. How can you find your life purpose?

   - a. By taking a nap

- b. By asking yourself the right questions
- c. By watching TV
- d. All of the above

4. Your perspective can change when you see your ideas on paper.

- a. True
- b. False

5. When brainstorming ideas for your life purpose, it's important to:

- a. Eat a snack
- b. Take a break
- c. Keep an open mind
- d. All of the above

6. What are some strategies that can help you find your life purpose?

- a. Reflecting
- b. Journaling
- c. Meditating
- d. All of the above

7. How can you determine which type of meditation is the most effective for you?

- a. Read books
- b. Experiment – try them out
- c. Ask your friend
- d. Ask your doctor

8. How can you strengthen your meditating skills?

- a. Practice
- b. Think about it
- c. Skip a week or two and then try again
- d. Watch TV

9. Figuring out the things that you're really good at can lead to discovering your life purpose.

- a. True
- b. False

10. Which strategy is more likely to be successful for making your purpose a part of your life?

- a. Redesign your whole life, starting tomorrow
- b. Make big, important changes immediately
- c. Make small changes that you can do each day
- d. Put off any decisions until you learn everything there is to know about life purposes

VII

Discovering Your Queenly Authenticity

Discover the power to live authentically. Learn to set priorities according to what's important to you. Develop the courage to be yourself around others and feel good about it. Practice listening to your intuition. And create a future in which you live the life you desire.

On Being Queen

*T*his last quest in your journey to being authentic will show you how you can set your life priorities around what you truly want and live your life accordingly. You'll see how to show your true self to the world and enjoy the results. Lastly, you'll see how to create a compelling future that truly excites you.

This first lesson in the module gives you some tips on living authentically:

Have there been times in your life when you felt you weren't acting like your true self? Maybe you were unsure of a situation or were lacking the confidence to reveal who you truly are.

Whatever your reason, you chose to hide your real self. ***Personal concealment places us into an emotionally unhealthy cycle. First, we feel unsure of ourselves and this causes us to act even less authentic in the future.*** We may even begin to wonder, "Who am I?"

Rather than spending time hiding from the world, you'll flourish by revealing your true self to others. Becoming more authentic in your interactions is definitely possible.

Commit to increasing your personal authenticity in these ways:

1. Monitor your feelings closely. *When you know and understand your own emotions, you'll be less likely to behave in ways that contrast with your feelings.*

- Mindfulness will help you tremendously in your quest to be more authentic.

- Stay in the moment and consider what is going on in your world in the present.

2. Give yourself time. If something happens and you're unsure of how to react or respond, it's okay to not react at all. Allow yourself some moments to consider the situation.

- If you feel pressure to respond, saying something like, "I'm not sure how to respond to that," can be your best line of action until you're more confident in your reaction.

3. Catch yourself being inauthentic. When you realize you've been less than honest in a given situation, it's okay to say, "Wait a minute. I changed my mind," or "Maybe I'm not as sure about this as I thought."

- *Remind yourself that you have permission to alter your response to anyone and anything at any time.* Then, choose a route that's more in line with how you honestly feel.

4. Notice what situations prompt you to be disingenuous. Being insincere or untruthful each time you're around your in-laws or your supervisor, for example, will reveal where your insecurities lie.

- Do some self-reflection to determine why you're behaving this way around that person or in that particular situation.

5. Be authentic with others to increase your level of confidence. The ability to be open and honest shows that you like and accept yourself and you're self-assured. *Avoid being afraid or too timid to show others who you really are.* Self-confidence goes a long way!

6. Realize that others truly appreciate you when you're authentic in behavior and comments. Think about how you feel when you're with someone who's consistently open with you. It feels comfortable and easy to be with someone you know you can trust. There's no tension or guesswork involved.

- If you keep this information in mind, you may find it a little easier to be authentic.

7. Show care and gentleness toward others. You might be thinking, "What's the connection between being caring and being authentic?" *If you go out of your way to be polite and kind to others, it will be a natural response to be authentic with them.*

- Once you realize that you hold their feelings in your hands, you'll know it's necessary to be gentle and honest with others.

When you expend a little bit of effort on relating to others truthfully and carefully, you'll gradually find that you like yourself more. **When you offer authenticity to others, it sets a wonderful example for those around you.** The more authentic you are, the richer the life you'll live.

In the next lesson, you'll discover how to set your life priorities, so you can design your life around what you love most.

Here's what you need to do today:

What situations tempt you to be insincere? Reflect on these situations. What can you do in these situations in the future to show your true feelings?

Login to Prince, Not Required and learn how liberating it is to live life on your own terms.

Setting Priorities Like a Queen

In this module, you're learning tips, tricks, and strategies on how to live authentically. A big part of living authentically is setting your life priorities. This lesson will explore life priorities and show you several benefits of figuring out what your life priorities are.

Every now and then, you may ponder the complexities and maybe even some chaos in your life. You might struggle to figure out what's next. Maybe you feel confused at times about which way to go. Have you thought about setting your life priorities to make your life easier?

When you're struggling to determine what's important to you, it's hard to make decisions. What will you do next? Where will you go for the evening? Who will you choose to pass the time with?

Feeling torn between two or more people, places and things is common if you haven't yet identified your priorities. After all, when you consider everything and everyone in your life as all-equal in terms of their "level" of importance, it's going to be tough to choose what to do next.

Setting your life priorities is a way of identifying what's most

important to you. Once you determine your priorities, you'll be pleased with the ease of making decisions and the serenity that comes with knowing you did the right thing.

Establishing priorities also gives you a clearer focus on how to allot your time. If you allot the bulk of your time to doing what's most important with the most important people in your life, ***you'll feel more fulfilled and satisfied with your life experiences.***

Common Life Priorities

What might your priorities be? The possibilities are endless. In the list below, you'll find many common priorities in no particular order. Feel free to use the list as inspiration to help you figure out your own priorities.

Family
 Finances
 Friends
 Extended family
 Work
 Hobbies
 Personal appearance
 Health and physical exercise/activities
 Nutritious eating
 "Alone-time" with partner
 Quality time with the children
 Playing games on the internet
 Talking on the phone
 Watching television

Example of a "Prioritized" Listing of Life Priorities

The whole idea of setting priorities is to put the many elements of your life into an order, with those that are most important to you at the top. ***Knowing your highest priority on the list is necessary in order to make focused, wise decisions that are right for you.***

Consider this next list, which is prioritized, as an example of someone's life priorities (in order).

1. Family
2. Alone-time with partner
3. Work
4. Health and physical exercise
5. Nutritious eating
6. Friends
7. Watching television
8. Personal appearance
9. Hobbies - movies and reading

Coming Up With Your Own Priorities

Setting your priorities in life may take time and effort. However, ***taking the time to reflect on your day-to-day life and determine what's on the top of your list will make your life so much easier.*** Once your priorities are clear to you, decisions on how to spend your time and with who will be a cinch.

Engaging in this exercise of figuring out your priorities might reveal some things that shock or surprise you.

For example, you might realize that you're spending most of your time hanging out with friends even though you feel that your family is more important. Or you aren't taking as much care with your kids as you thought you were.

Regardless of what you discover that you weren't expecting, setting your priorities now will help you limit or even remove the less-important elements of your life and enable you to focus more fully on what means the most to you.

You can live more joyfully by setting your life priorities. Knowing what's important to you and devoting your time to those things at the top of your list will ensure you experience an enriched and fulfilled life. Set your life priorities today.

To help you in your journey to authenticity, in the next lesson, I dare you to be yourself!

Here's what you need to do today:

Take the time to reflect on what is the most important thing to you. This is your top priority. Write this priority in your journal. Determine one way in which you can start incorporating this priority more into your daily life.

Dare to Be the Queen You Want to Be

*P*reviously in this module, you've set your life priorities and learned some strategies for living authentically. Now, we dare you to be yourself!

Are you comfortable being yourself in all situations? If you're like most people, you're 90% yourself when you're with close friends, 50% yourself with casual acquaintances, and hide yourself from strangers. ***Being your true self in all settings and situations is scary, but ultimately empowering and relaxing.*** Imagine the relief you'll experience.

You no longer have to worry about the perceptions of others. You can just be yourself and feel satisfied with that.

Be yourself and take back control of your life:

1. **Meditate.** Meditation quiets the part of you that judges and labels everything around you. Gain some insight into the real you by meditating regularly.

2. **Tell the truth.** When you're truthful, you reveal yourself. Be honest about your mistakes and shortcomings.

3. **Be unique.** The true you isn't exactly like everyone else. What music do you listen to when you're alone? How do you dress? Do you keep the unique parts to yourself or are you willing to share them with the world?

4. **Notice your crutches and get rid of them.** Rocky road ice cream? Mindless internet surfing? A double vanilla café latte? *Using crutches to deal with boredom, anxiety or uncertainty is blocking you from seeing the truth.*

- What is the purpose of a particular crutch? Stop using it and see for yourself.

5. **Examine the areas in your life that feel inauthentic.** When and where do you feel like you're lacking authenticity? Often it will be during interactions with strangers, first dates, new social experiences, and more formal occasions.

- A lack of authenticity can also occur when you spend time with your parents and siblings. They just don't seem to want you to change, so you fall back into your old roles.

- *Think about the times you're inauthentic and ask yourself why.*

6. **Spend your time on things you enjoy.** What do you really

enjoy? Do you play on the softball league so you'll fit in? Would you rather be taking rumba lessons? Spend your free time on the things that you're most passionate about.

7. **Do one thing you want to do but are afraid to try.** The people at the office might laugh if you take up the cello or take an acting class. *However, secretly, they'll be jealous that you have the nerve to do something unconventional.* Everyone you know is stifled and bored. You can rise above all of that.

8. **Give your opinion.** Not necessarily all of the time, but give your opinion if it won't hurt anyone. Going to see a movie with some friends? Tell them the movie you'd most like to see. The family wants to go to the public pool or the park? Let your opinion be known. Wife wants to know if she looks fat in her dress? Be smart.

9. **Get outside.** An indoor environment is unnatural. The air is heated or cooled. The lighting is artificial. You can't see the sun, hear the birds, or feel the grass beneath your feet. Get yourself into a more natural environment and you'll find it easier to be authentic.

10. **Strengthen your boundaries.** *Where your boundaries are weak, your true self is being smothered.* These are the places we allow others to determine the rules and set the frame. You'll know these places by the high amounts of energy they drain from you.

Overcome your need to fit in and impress others. No matter what you do, some people will be impressed and others won't. Why worry about it? *You're an amazing person.* Allow yourself to be that person each and every day.

Do you find it hard to be yourself? The next couple of lessons help you in this regard with some tips to help you reveal your true personality and express your true feelings to others.

Here's what you need to do today:

Today, do one thing you've always wanted to do but were too afraid to try!

10 Easy Ways to Reveal Your Inner Queen

*I*n the last lesson, did you find it challenging when you tried out living authentically? If so, you'll be glad to learn the strategies in this lesson that help you reveal your true personality to the world.

It's possible to enhance your personality and your ability to share it more authentically with others. ***You'll form stronger and more meaningful relationships if you're able to be yourself.*** Maybe you've been too reserved in the past to let others see the real you. You can change that by taking the bull by the horns.

Show the world who you really are:

1. **Improve your conversational skills.** You can't reveal your true personality if you don't communicate effectively. Conversational skills are important to have and influence multiple areas of your life. You also build your personality by conversing with others. You can't know everything, so learning from others is one way to grow and become more interesting.

- Poor communication skills result in being misunderstood. Your personality will be misunderstood, too.

2. **Share your opinion.** Have you ever spoken to someone that didn't have an opinion? It's boring. Many of us keep our opinions to ourselves in an effort not to offend, but it has a negative effect. Interesting people have opinions. Be brave enough to share yours.

- Make a pact with yourself to always have an opinion. When you're asked about your movie or dinner preference, give an answer other than, "I don't care" or "I don't know".

3. **Be positive.** A negative outlook brings out the worst in all of us. Put your best foot forward by being upbeat. Being around others that complain and see the dark side of life is tiresome. Be uplifting and allow your real personality to shine.

4. **Be yourself.** Just like your mom said. Pretending to be someone you're not is dishonest. It's also hard on your self-esteem. Embrace the parts of you that are unique and share them with others. Some people will like you while others do not. That's true regardless of your personality.

5. **Engage in your interests.** Make the time to pursue the activities that appeal to you. Go mountain climbing, learn to play the banjo, or volunteer with the homeless. When you're living your life to the fullest, people can see you at your best. You'll enjoy life much more, too.

6. **Become a better listener.** Listening has several benefits. It will lower your anxiety, make the other person feel important, and create a connection.

- The better the connection, the more likely you'll be to show your true colors. You learn much more while you're listening.

7. **Increase your social circle.** Expose yourself to new opinions and cultures. Meet new people and watch your personality blossom. You'll become stagnant by hanging out with the same people all of the time.

8. **Be respectful.** You're a respectful person and have integrity, even if you haven't been showing it lately. You deserve the same from others. Show people the best you have to offer and you'll inspire others to follow suit.

9. **Relax.** If you're not relaxed, you're protecting yourself. If you're protecting yourself, you're not being your true self. Be more carefree. See the humorous side of life. You true personality is revealed when you're happy and light.

10. **Read.** Develop greater knowledge about the world and the things that matter to you. Become an expert on the topics that fascinate you. Your personality will grow and reveal itself more completely.

Do your friends and family know the real you? Does it take new acquaintances a long time to know you well? Let the world see your true personality. ***Build your personality and share it with others.*** Your relationships and self-esteem will improve. You'll also experience a sense of peace. There's no reason to keep yourself a secret!

In the next lesson, you'll explore another area that may be challenging you in trying to live authentically: expressing your true feelings.

Here's what you need to do today:

Share your opinion. For the rest of this week, have an opinion about anything that is asked about. Avoid statements such as, "I don't know," or "I don't care." Let others start getting used to hearing a real opinion from you.

Grab the Dragon by the Horns

~~~~~~~~

Express Your Feelings

*I*n this module about living authentically, you previously learned some strategies for revealing your true personality. This lesson helps you find the courage to express your true feelings as well.

Life is full of situations where it can be difficult to say what we really think but silence sometimes comes at a high cost.

In a recent article in the British newspaper The Guardian, *a nurse reported that failing to express our true emotions is one of the most common deathbed regrets.*

Read on to discover the major benefits of speaking your mind and constructive ways to get started.

Benefits of Expressing Your Emotions

1. **Lead a fuller life.** Dare to take on difficult issues. You'll learn more about yourself, your loved ones and the world around you. Taking on more challenges will help you discover your true potential.

2. **Become more authentic**. If you habitually suppress your true feelings, you may become unfamiliar with them yourself. Get to know the real you and accept yourself for who you are.

3. **Banish your fears.** *Fear and anxiety build up when we try to shelter ourselves from difficult truths rather than facing them directly*. When you see yourself successfully negotiating a disagreement with your boss, you'll feel more confident in your abilities.

4. **Improve your relationships.** Clearing the air promptly can keep resentments from building up. Ask your spouse to share in more of the housework rather than feeling like a martyr.

5. **Liberate others.** Courage is contagious. Your willingness to be direct and honest makes it easier for others to do the same.

Techniques for Expressing Your Emotions

1. **Clarify your intentions.** Everyone benefits when we devote ourselves to promoting the common good. It beats worrying about being comfortable or universally popular.

2. **Consider the risks involved.** There may still be situations in

240

which you need to choose restraint. Maybe you have valid concerns about an office policy but know that your supervisor is unlikely to be receptive to suggestions.

3. **Take accountability for your own emotions.** State your feelings in a way that avoids putting the blame on others. *Recognize that your unpleasant feelings have more to do with your mindset rather than external events.*

4. **Start out small.** It's okay to proceed gradually. Talk with your best friend about how her showing up late for appointments affects you. Soon you'll be able to approach people who may be less directly concerned with your well being.

5. **Practice regularly.** Like any skill, open communications improve the more you practice. Notice daily opportunities to speak up so you'll be in shape when more difficult conflicts come along.

6. **Remain tactful.** Even when you need to confront difficult truths, you can pick a setting and language that will make the message more palatable. If tempers are already flaring, give yourselves time to calm down and speak privately. *Try making requests rather than demanding changes.*

7. **Respect other's boundaries.** Just because you've decided to become more forthright, other people may still have different priorities. Unless someone's welfare is in serious danger, be sensitive to the topics they may prefer to leave untouched.

8. **Listen intentionally.** On the other hand, you may find that others welcome the opportunity to be candid. Give people your full attention. Show that you're attuned to their concerns. If you feel overwhelmed by what you're hearing, ask for time to reflect before

continuing the discussion.

9. **Share good news too.** Sometimes we shy away from pleasant feelings as well as the unpleasant ones. Get in the habit of handing out more compliments. Let people know how their kind acts improve your life and how much you care about them.

If you want to live life to the fullest, get in touch with your true feelings and bring them out into the open. You'll enrich your own experiences and empower those around you to do the same.

In living authentically, it's important to be honest with others and yourself, too. The next lesson shares some tips about presenting yourself honestly.

Here's what you need to do today:

Start out small and share good news too. Today, share your good feelings and give out at least 5 sincere compliments.

Queens are Honest, but Kind!

*P*reviously, you learned some strategies to show the world your personality and express your feelings. However, authenticity is more than being honest with the world. It's also about being honest with yourself.

There are many advantages to being truly authentic. ***Most importantly, you'll no longer feel the need to change your words and actions to impress others.*** You can relax and be yourself.

Embrace authenticity and present yourself honestly:

1. **Give up the need to appear perfect.** Excellent is good enough. But seriously, when you don't need to appear perfect, you're in the position to be honest. No one can be perfect and honest at the same time. Avoid putting on a show for the rest of the world. You'll only feel bad about yourself later.

- It's okay to be less than spectacular. ***Be the best at being yourself.***

2. **Know your values and live by them.** If you know your values and live by them consistently, you're already doing well in the authentic department.

- Make a list of your values and determine the five that are most important to you. Are you living your life according to these values? Would it be obvious to others that you hold these values?

- Decide to make your decisions based upon your values. Be willing to share your values with others.

3. **Notice when you're not being authentic.** It's not easy to be authentic all the time. *You might find yourself transforming based on the situation.* A first date is a good example. Are you being authentic or pretending to be someone you're not?

- Take note of those times your authenticity starts to wane

4. **Know your goals.** What do you want out of life? Do you know? Are you willing to let others know? By knowing your goals, you can you live your life accordingly.

- Make a list of your short-term and long-term goals. How well do they align with your values?

5. **What are your defining characteristics?** Describe yourself honestly. Now ask yourself if a casual acquaintance would describe you the same way? How about someone that knows you well? How about your closest friend?

- How many people know you well? If there aren't many, ask yourself why. If you're living authentically, it should be easy for someone to develop an accurate opinion of you.

- What are your "negative" characteristics? Are you impatient or messy? Are you willing to allow others to see these characteristics or do you attempt to hide them?

6. **Tell the truth.** *If you're being authentic, why would you need to lie?* This pertains especially to anything you say about yourself. Admit your mistakes, weaknesses, and frailties. Share your opinions honestly and freely.

7. **Simplify your life.** Get rid of everything that's extraneous. What you choose to keep will be representative of your preferences and your true self. Find your true essence by stripping away the non-essential. Start with the clothes you never wear, the things you never use, and the activities you don't enjoy. Only keep the things that mean the most to you.

8. **Do what you say you'll do.** Keep your word and follow through on your promises. You'll feel more congruent, and others will view you as more congruent. When your words and actions match, you're demonstrating authenticity.

Life becomes easier when you're living authentically. *You'll no*

longer feel the exhaustion that comes with constantly changing your opinions, attitudes, and personality to please others. You'll no longer feel the need to protect yourself from others. Be authentic with your thoughts, words, and actions. Invest the time in yourself and learn to be free.

Trusting in yourself also makes it easier to be authentic. The next lesson shares ideas for trusting yourself.

Here's what you need to do today:

What are your defining characteristics? In your journal, describe yourself honestly. Now ask yourself if a casual acquaintance would describe you the same way? How about someone that knows you well? How about your closest friend?

If your descriptions from the various people are different, why is that? Are you presenting yourself honestly?

The Power of Your Inner Voice

$$\mathcal{Q}\mathcal{C}\mathcal{Q}$$

*I*n the last lesson, we looked at presenting yourself honestly. In this lesson, we'll explore how your inner voice is also important to living authentically.

Your inner voice expresses the honest feelings of your true self and is the source of your inspiration, creativity, and intuition. By listening to your inner voice, you can gain insight into what makes you happy and unhappy. You can also gain the power to transform your life into one that is more vibrant and fulfilling.

Unfortunately, most of us don't listen our inner voices because we're too busy juggling all of the responsibilities and demands of our daily lives.

The good news is that regardless of how busy or hectic your life may be, there are ways to filter out the distractions so you can hear your inner voice. As you reconnect with your true self, you can use that voice to guide you to the things that will bring more joy, progress, and peace into your life.

Use these strategies to filter out the noise of daily life and

harness the power of your inner voice:

1. **Make time for reflection.** One way to get in touch with your inner voice is to set aside a regular time for self-reflection. Think about the things in your life that are going well and that make you happy, as well as the things that you're dissatisfied with.

- It's important to be honest and open with yourself as you reflect on your life, so that you can hear your true inner voice. ***Ignore the critical voices from the past and avoid letting society tell you how to live your life.***

- Reflect on how you truly feel about the direction your life is taking.

- Seek out a place and time for your moments of self-reflection where you can be alone and uninterrupted for at least 30 minutes.

- Choose a place where you can relax, such as a sofa or bed. If you find it easier to practice self-reflection by taking a relaxing nature walk, performing some gentle stretching exercises, practicing controlled breathing, or doing yoga poses, this is fine as well.

- Write down the thoughts, impressions, and dreams that emerge during your self-reflection time. Once you begin to practice self-reflection on a regular basis, you'll start to hear your true inner voice. ***It's helpful to record the insight that you gain.***

- Making lists, keeping a journal, or even sharing your impressions with a close friend can help you to focus on the areas that you want to change in order to bring more happiness and joy into your life.

2. **Learn to trust your inner voice and take action on your discoveries.** As you gain experience listening to your inner voice and seeking clues in your dreams, learn to trust that voice.

- It's okay to begin small, but *make time each day to do something that you truly enjoy.* Each step that you take will put you one step closer to living the life that you see in your dreams.

- Just as you are working to incorporate more things into your daily life that bring you true joy, *reduce or eliminate those tasks and habits that bring you down.* As time passes, you may find that you need to move on to a new career or abandon certain relationships.

- Let go of things and people that drain your energy and prevent you from being truly happy.

While it will take some time, practicing self-reflection on a regular basis can teach you how to hear your true inner voice and use it to guide you to true authenticity and greater happiness and joy in your life.

In the next lesson, you'll learn some strategies for being proud to cultivate your own originality.

Here's what you need to do today:

Make time for reflection. Set aside a regular reflecting time of at least 30 minutes. In your first reflection, reflect on the direction that your life is heading. Do you see it unfolding authentically?

What changes would you like to make to increase your authenticity? Plan these changes in your journal and take action to get started on them.

The Courage of Originality

*n the last lesson, you learned about listening to your inner voice. Your inner voice is honest, and reveals the real you to yourself. In living authentically, you want to encourage bringing out the real you, especially the parts about you that are unique.

Having the courage to be original really means **being brave enough to be yourself.** Certainly this can seem daunting and frightening, because to really live as you are means opening yourself up to the judgement of others. Usually, we shield ourselves from others to some extent.

Each of us is uniquely valuable. So why hide the truth of who you are?

Imagine what it might be like if everyone truly knew you, inside and out, what wonderful things you're capable of, and how fully human you are, just like them.

There can be a great, false comfort in conforming and keeping your head down. But you sacrifice ever knowing your true potential. And you risk boredom; when the path is fully laid out for you, there's no adventure.

Living with originality takes some courage for sure, but the rewards far outweigh the penalties of hiding your inner self.

Being original has a lot of perks:

1. **Greater fulfillment and personal satisfaction.** Life has more meaning when it's 100% authentic.

2. **Increased charisma.** People will find you more interesting and pay attention to you more. Authentic people are attractive to pretty much everyone.

3. **Greater ability to take risks and be creative.** Your life will have more depth and you'll experience more success in every part of your life.

4. **Opportunity.** *By being original, you stand a chance to change the world. And regardless of what you do, you'll surely be remembered.* Only unique people do great things. Average people do average things.

Try these ideas to cultivate your originality:

1. **Be aware of who you are inside.** This may take some thought, especially if you spend all day working and all night watching television. Regularly spend quiet time with yourself. Contemplate who you are and what you stand for.

2. **Express yourself freely.** Give your opinions without judging yourself, especially when you're asked for them. Let people know what you think without being unkind. *Allow yourself to have your own style,* whether it's your taste in music, your profession, or just what to wear today.

3. **Avoid worrying about others' opinions.** *The big secret is that they're probably worried about what you think of them.* Chances are good that nobody is spending much time thinking about any of us. And there's nothing more attractive to others than someone that moves through the world confidently and without apology.

- Just be yourself and let the chips fall where they may. *You'll be surprised how easy it is once you try it.* It's analogous to being afraid of the dark; there's simply nothing there to fear.

Consider famous people like Abraham Lincoln, Albert Einstein, Marie Curie, and others. Do you know of another person who is anything like any of them? *They're originals.*

People who conform can never really stand out unless they're in extraordinary circumstances. Maybe you're not the next Albert Einstein, but *how will you ever know* if you decide to continue selling shoes all your life even though you want to quit and study physics?

Being original is about having the courage to be yourself and letting the world know who you are. This isn't always easy, but it's necessary to truly experience the depth of your life.

Have the courage to be unique! You'll live in an intensely fulfilled way and you'll be remembered long after you're gone.

The next lesson finishes your journey toward authenticity with helping you to create a compelling future based on your unique, true self and what's important to you.

Here's what you need to do today:

Reflect on how you are unique. How can you bring out your unique qualities? In your journal, write down your plans for bringing out this part of you.

A Queen's Unlimited Resources

[decorative flourish]

Now that you've learned to live authentically, this last part of your journey enables you to create a compelling future based on what YOU want in your life.

Have you ever wanted to do something, but discouraged yourself because you believed you lacked the necessary resources to be successful? They might include a lack of sufficient time, money, education, support, or experience.

Interestingly, a lack of resources is rarely an issue if you're truly committed! Avoid allowing a current lack of resources discourage you.

It's easy to get started on any venture without any resources. In time, resources can be found when needed. Even the largest businesses had humble beginnings.

Consider the power of believing you have unlimited resources:

1. **What would you choose to accomplish if you had unlimited resources?** Take a few minutes to consider how you would live your life if you had everything you needed. Would you go back to school? Start your own company? Become a philanthropist? Own an island? It's easy to see that your options are unlimited. Think big.

- This can be an excellent way to determine your life's purpose. *If all obstacles were removed, what would you choose to do?*

2. **Whom would you have in your life?** Would you be alone or married? How many friends would you have? Describe your friends. Describe your neighbors. How many children would you have? If you dream of owning your own business, describe your employees and clients.

3. **Where would you live?** Would you stay put or move to the beach? How many homes would you own? What color would your dining room be? Consider the geographical location and the actual dwelling. There are hundreds of castles for sale at any time. You'll need a butler, though.

4. **What would your typical day entail?** What time would you get out of bed? What would you do first? How would you spend your day? How would your evening be spent? How much free time would you have and how would you spend it? Whom would you see? Would you play golf every Thursday? Would you race cars on the weekend?

5. **Now that you know what you should be doing, how can you make it happen?** Few of us have a surplus of resources, but there is always a first step that can be taken.

- The first step might entail looking at the educational offerings in your area or seeking a higher-paying job. Maybe it's finally time to take the drum lessons you thought were silly. There's still time to be a rock star.
- *As you progress, your understanding and your resources will grow.* Oprah Winfrey went from wearing potato sacks to school to hosting her own morning show. Now she's frequently listed as one the richest women in the world. You probably didn't grow up having to wear potato sacks as dresses and your dreams are likely smaller. Consider that.

6. **Pretending you have unlimited resources can also be used to find solutions to challenges.** By imagining you have unlimited resources, you can open your mind to all the possible solutions. It's possible you'll find a solution that requires additional resources, but give yourself a chance to make it work.

Those with unlimited resources can still struggle, so having unlimited resources isn't a guarantee. Avoid believing that abundant resources are a cure to your struggles. Remember that many of the most successful people in the world started at the very bottom with no resources.

You probably don't have unlimited resources. *However, supposing that you have unlimited resources can help to determine your life's purpose, your dream existence, and create a new set of solutions.* Imagining that your resources are plentiful will open new possibilities.

You're limiting yourself right now. What would you do with unlimited resources?

Why not start by making your bucket list? You'll find tips for making your perfect bucket list in the online course.

Here's what you need to do today:

Make your bucket list, plan your exciting future, and relish the joy of living authentically!

Looking at the Queen in the Mirror

*T*his module started with some tips for living authentically and then guided you through solutions to particular challenges that you may encounter in your efforts to incorporate authenticity into your life.

Learn how to set your life priorities in accordance with what's important to you personally.

Discover the importance – and the joy – of showing the real you to the world. Try out the tips that make it easier for you to express your feelings. Learn to trust your own instincts. And see how to bring yourself new opportunities by proudly presenting your unique qualities and ideas as opposed to just conforming to what everyone else does.

Your journey to authenticity ends with a vision of your exciting future. Follow the steps to create goals based on your own desires.Make your bucket list. Design a plan that fulfills everything you've learned about yourself in eight different areas of your life, from what type of home you want, to your career, relationships, intellectual pursuits, and more.

It has been a pleasure to guide you through these steps to authenticity! I wish you the very best as you move forward and experience the joys of living an authentic life.

Self-Reflection Exercises:

Queen, you're at the finish line. Complete this modules quiz and then move on to designing your Fairytale Blueprint ' What Do You Want: Designing A Plan For Your Life'.

It will help you use what you've learned in this course to live authentically by designing a plan for your life based on your own hopes, dreams, passions, and life purpose.

Queenly Authenticity Quiz

1. Rather than spending time hiding from the world, you'll flourish by revealing __[what]__ to others.

- a. Your bank account balance
- b. Your finest jewelry
- c. Your true self
- d. All of the above

2. Which strategy increases your personal authenticity?

- a. Monitor your feelings closely
- b. Notice which situations cause you to be insincere
- c. Catch yourself being inauthentic
- d. All of the above

3. What is a way of identifying the things and ideas that are most important to you?

- a. Setting your life priorities
- b. Taking a nap
- c. Increasing your confidence
- d. Strengthening your self-discipline

4. Where your boundaries are weak, your true self is being smothered.

- a. True
- b. False

5. Which strategy is an easy way to reveal your true personality?

- a. Share your opinion
- b. Engage in your interests
- c. Become an expert on the topics that fascinate you
- d. All of the above

6. What is likely to happen when you try to shelter yourself from a difficult truth?

- a. You can happily go on your way
- b. Fear and anxiety build up
- c. It's easier to be authentic
- d. You reduce stress

7. Authenticity is more than being honest with the world. So what else is it?

- a. It's only showing your best self
- b. It's being honest with yourself
- c. It's a stressful way to live
- d. All of the above

8. If your life is really busy and hectic, you can't tune in to your inner voice.

- a. True
- b. False

9. Which way of living is more fun, fulfilling, and gives you a chance to change the world?

- a. Being an original, showing the world your unique self
- b. Conforming to every norm so you don't have to worry about someone thinking poorly of you
- c. Ensuring you remain within your comfort zone
- d. Following all the rules

10. In living authentically, which of the following activities might be included in your regular routines?

- a. Making up stories to impress your date

- b. Watching TV
- c. Telling your spouse you have to work late so you can go out with your friends to have authentic adventures
- d. All of the above

VIII

My Fairy Tale Blueprint

What Do You Want?
Designing a Plan for Your Life

Getting Started

Having a Fairy Tale Blueprint (Life Plan) brings focus and determination to your life. After all, if you're looking at your Life Plan occasionally, you'll be more likely to follow through with your plans and achieve life goals. Use this workbook to write your own Life Plan. **When you see your Life Plan, you'll be exhilarated, stimulated, and look forward to getting on with living the life you truly want.**

Review the Points to Ponder questions related to 8 life areas. Rather than write your answers to those questions, just think about each one. Next, move on to write your answers to the bolded questions in the spaces provided about what you want in life. Finally, write the steps you'll take to achieve your wants/goals. You've got your Fairy Tale Blueprint!

My Fairy Tale
Blueprint

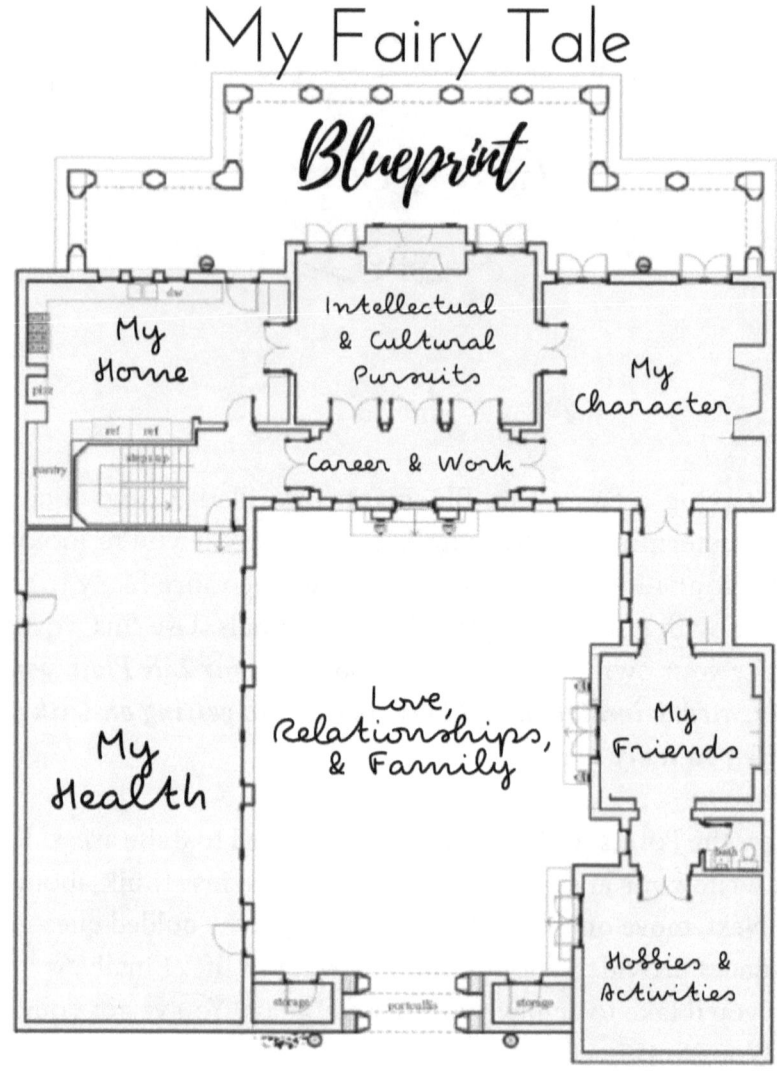

Turn the page to start designing your very own Fairy Tale Blueprint!

Your Home

o you live in the location you want?

Do you reside in the type of home (apartment, house, or condo) that you desire?

Does your home reflect who you are and what you prefer the way you'd like it to?

Your desired location to live is:

Type of residence you desire:

Changes you want to make inside your home, such as room arrangements and how the space is used:

Steps you'll take to get what you want related to your home:

1.

2.

3.

4.

5.

Your Health

*H*ow is your health?

Are you in the physical condition you would opt to be in?

Do you look like you thought you would at this point in life?

Are you pleased about how you take care of yourself?

Are you as active physically as you want to be?

How do you handle emotionally challenging situations?

Would you like to resolve old psychological issues but just haven't gotten around to doing it?

What, if any, changes do you want to make regarding your physical health?

Steps you'll follow to accomplish those changes:

1.

2.

3.

What do you want regarding your emotional health?

Steps you'll follow to achieve your goals regarding your emotional health:

1.

2.

Your Career and Work

*I*s the career you're working in now the type of job and work you'd opt for?

Do you have a clear plan for the future in terms of what you want to do jobwise?

Is there anything you wish to change about your career/job? Write it here:

Steps you'll take to achieve these changes related to your job:

1.

2.

3.

Your Love, Relationships, and Family

If you're in a special relationship, are you happy about it?

Is it fulfilling your emotional needs?

Are you happy in your family situation?

Do you provide the type of parenting that you always believed you would?

Do you spend adequate quality time with your family?

If you have a love relationship, do you want to change anything about it?

If so, what?

If you don't have a love relationship but want one, you can write it here.

Steps you'll take to achieve what you want regarding a love relationship:

1.

2.

3.

4.

Do you have or want a family?

What, if any, changes do you wish to make regarding you and your family?

Steps you'll take to achieve what you want related to your family:

1.

2.

3.

4.

Your Friends

Would you choose your current friends all over again?

Do you learn from them, share with them, laugh with them, and cry with them?

Are your friendships at the level of relating that you want?

Are you satisfied with everything related to your friends? Write down anything you'd like to change regarding friendships here.

How will you achieve these changes? Steps you'll take to achieve what you want related to your friendships:

1.

2.

3.

Your Character

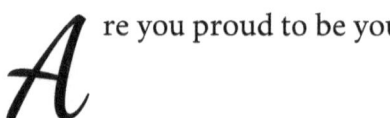

*A*re you proud to be you?

Do you have the character traits you admire?

If you want to work to strengthen your character in any way, write about specifically what you want to change:

Steps to achieve these goals:

1.

2.

3.

Your Hobbies and Activities

How are you spending your spare time?

Do you do activities that interest you, that you're passionate about, or that you can't wait to do next time?

If you're pleased with how you spend your spare time, that's great. Or use this space to write about the changes you want to make regarding hobbies and activities.

Steps to achieve your goals regarding hobbies and activities:

1.

2.

3.

Your Intellectual and Cultural Pursuits

D o you pursue the intellectual topics and cultural events that interest you?

Do you wish to pursue further intellectual and cultural pursuits?

Steps for developing more intellectual and cultural pursuits:

1.

2.

3.

How do you feel about the Life Plan you just created?

Did you include everything you truly want in life?

Congratulations on your efforts to plan and live the life you've always wanted!

*"**He who fails to plan plans to fail.**" ~Proverb*

IX

A Journey Completed

*This journey was a long one, but you made it!
The greatest time that we can ever spend, is on ourselves.
Please feel free to write me and let me know your thoughts
after working through this book and the online course. I
love feedback and I love hearing about all the wonderful
changes that my fellow Queens have enacted in their lives.*

*Really! Pen me a note and send it to
princenotrequired@gmail.com*

*XoXo all my support
Abiegail Rose*

Logging in to the Course

S tep 1 - Visit: www.princenotrequired.com

Step 2 - Click: Grab Your Seat in the Free Masterclass

Step 3 - Enroll in Class

Step 4 - Get your class FREE with code: noprinceneeded

Welcome!

About the Author

I am a romance novelist, motivational author, and public speaker. I have written numerous books and spoken in front of thousands of people. I still get nervous with each new release and each time I stand on a stage.

My goal is to touch the life of every woman I come in contact with. Whether it's by making her believe in love again, or most importantly to believe in herself again.

You can connect with me on:
- http://www.princenotrequired.com
- http://facebook.com/authorabiegailrose
- http://goodreads.com/abiegailrose
- http://instagram.com/princenotrequired

Subscribe to my newsletter:
- http://linktr.ee/sultryreads